2-5-75

ommunity Service rders

K. Pease, P. Durkin, I. Earnshaw,
ayne, J. Thorpe

LONDON: HER MAJESTY'S STATIONERY OFFICE 1975

ISBN 0 11 340669 x

FOREWORD

The Criminal Justice Act 1972 introduced a number of new measures for dealing with offenders. The Home Office Research Unit is studying the operation of several of these measures and this report – a study of community service – enshrines the first results.

The community service scheme was brought into experimental operation in six probation and after-care areas early in 1973: the Unit evaluated it during the first 18 months of its operation and reached the conclusion, recorded in this report, that the scheme is viable. In consequence, probation and after-care committees have been invited by the Home Office to provide community service schemes throughout England and Wales as soon as practicable after 1 April 1975 (subject to the availability of local resources).

The report describes the efforts made by all concerned, and in particular the probation and after-care service in the six experimental areas, to give a fair test to this novel form of penal treatment. The use made of it by the courts, the offenders they chose to apply it to, the help given by local voluntary and official agencies in making appropriate tasks available, the reactions of some of the offenders, and some of the difficulties encountered are all examined. One-year reconviction rates of offenders ordered to perform community service during the scheme's first year of operation in the six experimental areas will be calculated in mid-1975.

I. J. CROFT
Head of the Research Unit

February 1975

ACKNOWLEDGEMENTS

Thanks are due to all those in the probation and after-care services of Durham, Inner London, Kent, Nottingham, Shropshire and South-West Lancashire who provided us with information while we were collecting the data on which this report is founded: in particular we are grateful to the officers then responsible for the community service scheme. Acknowledgement should also be made of the extensive help given to us by our clerical officer and typists, who have consistently worked cheerfully to the tightest of schedules.

K. PEASE
P. DURKIN
I. EARNSHAW
D. PAYNE
J. THORPE

CONTENTS

TABLES

CHAPTER 1

Background to the Community Service Scheme

The legislation

Section 15 of the Criminal Justice Act 1972*([1]) empowered courts to order offenders to perform unpaid work as a service to the community. The provision followed recommendations by the Advisory Council on the Penal System in their report, *Non-custodial and Semi-custodial Penalties*, published in 1970 and known as the Wootton report([2]). A Home Office working group then considered 'the practical issues raised by a scheme of community service by offenders and what formal arrangement seems suited to give effect to it', and made suggestions for implementing (with some modifications) the Wootton report proposals.

In the second reading debate on the Criminal Justice Bill, the then Home Secretary (Mr. Reginald Maudling) said 'I was attracted from the start by the idea that people who have committed minor offences would be better occupied doing a service to their fellow citizens than sitting alongside others in a crowded gaol. . . . This will, of course, have to be a voluntary choice of the individual concerned for a number of reasons; after all if it is not done voluntarily the work will not be good. The alternative will be to go to gaol.'([3]).

The community service order provisions proved uncontroversial. In Committee, the Parliamentary Under Secretary of State said 'only when one has attempted it will one know whether community service can play a part in our penal system. I know that it is the personal wish of the Home Secretary that not only should it work, but that it should be a type of order which the courts may come to use freely and one which they will turn to as an alternative to short custodial sentences as a means of making people pay for their offences rather than merely spend a short time, of a probably not very reformative nature, in an overcrowded local prison'([4]).

A community service order can be made in respect of an offender convicted of an offence punishable with imprisonment provided he is aged 17 or over and consents. The number of hours to be worked, not less than 40 or more than 240, are specified in the order and must normally be completed within one year of the date of the order. Community service work arrangements should, so far as is possible, not conflict with the offender's work, educational or religious commitments. A court cannot make an order unless (i) arrangements for community service have been made in the petty sessions area where the offender will reside; (ii) the court is satisfied, after considering a probation officer's report about the offender and his circumstances, that he is a suitable person to per-

---

* now s.14, Powers of Criminal Courts Act 1973

form work under such an order; and (iii) the court is also satisfied that provision can be made for him to do so.

Arrangements for community service are a function of probation and after-care committees. Probation officers allocate offenders to tasks provided by local voluntary agencies, local authority departments and the service itself, and exercise general oversight of the offenders' compliance with the orders. In 1973, the community service scheme was introduced experimentally in six areas: Durham, Inner London, Kent, Nottinghamshire, Shropshire and South West Lancashire (with local government reorganisation on 1 April 1974 the South West Lancashire probation area ceased to be, but Merseyside probation and after-care service took over operation of the scheme).

The Wootton report (paragraph 63) urged that, 'as with any new penal experiment, provision for systematic study of the working of the community service project should be incorporated in the scheme from the outset.' The Home Office Research Unit undertook this study.

Aims and methods of the research

The aim of the research was to provide background data to inform a decision about the viability of the community service scheme and the consequent decision about its extension. The research began in August 1972, and ended in August 1974 apart from a subsequent examination of reconviction rates of those in respect of whom orders were made in 1973, and completion of a study of the characteristics that make offenders suitable for community service. Specifically the aims of the research were to describe:

(1) the background to the scheme and its rationale (Chapter 1).

(2) the criteria probation officers appear to use in making judgements of an offender's suitability for community service (Chapter 2). The following methods were used to assess these criteria:

   (i)   ascertaining views about suitability in each probation and after-care area;

   (ii) conducting a sentencing exercise with main-grade probation officers in three of the probation and after-care areas;

   (iii) analysing the content of social inquiry reports in which community service is considered.

(3) the offenders ordered to perform community service (Chapter 3). The following methods were used:

   (i)   recording information from files in community service offices;

   (ii) obtaining criminal record information on persons subject to community service orders.

(4) the conduct of the community service scheme, including the relationship between recommendations for a community service order and eventual disposal by the court; the work done by offenders, in what company it was done and who supervised it, when and for how long it was done, and how long it took to termination; what was the outcome of orders, in terms of success, breach etc (Chapters 3 & 4). The methods used were:

(i)   completion of a research form each time a probation officer, when writing a social inquiry report, considered a community service order, whether he did so on his own initiative or on the court's instruction;

(ii)   participant observation at community service offices and work sites;

(iii)   intensive interviews with the probation officers having day-to-day responsibility for the community service scheme;

(iv)   recording information from files in community service offices;

(v)   asking probation officers with responsibility for the scheme in the six experimental areas to say which completed orders they regard as 'successes' or 'cases which have given them satisfaction'.

(5) the attitudes and opinions expressed about community service by relevant groups or individuals (Chapter 5). The methods used were:

(i)   intensive interviews with the probation officer in each area who had direct responsibility for the community service scheme;

(ii)   a postal survey of the attitudes of a sample of main-grade and senior probation officers drawn from the experimental areas;

(iii)   analysis of the words used by sentencers when making community service orders;

(iv)   formal interviews with a sample of offenders doing community service;

(v)   analysis of one area's dossier of contacts with potential work-providing agencies;

(vi)   content analysis of press-cuttings on community service, obtained through a press-cutting agency covering many of the 'newspapers, periodicals and consumer magazines published in the United Kingdom'.

The precise form of the research was largely dictated by what seemed to be the most important issues at the time. Certain lines of research proved abortive. For example, the Research Unit intended to examine the reasons for withdrawal of work-providing agencies, and prepared a form for this purpose. However, few agencies withdrew, and those that did were unwilling to communicate their reasons to the Research Unit. Also, it was intended to examine

3

the amount of informal casework help being given to those on community service, but it soon became apparent that it would be virtually impossible to gain any accurate estimate of this, because probation officers in offices other than the community service office would by no means always record such contacts.

Comments on evaluation

The Wootton Committee report([2]), in recommending (para 63) systematic study of the scheme from the outset, said 'we would emphasise the dangers of drawing premature conclusions from early experience. We hope, therefore, that the most careful consideration will be given to the design of an appropriate research project'.

It is possible to distinguish between two types of evaluation of a new penal measure. The first attempts to describe the salient features of the operation of a scheme, so as to provide a basis for a decision about the scheme's viability and about possible directions of change which might be desirable. It is also useful as a vehicle for passing on some of the lessons learned during the scheme's early days of operation. The second type of evaluation attempts to show whether a measure meets its primary aim, which in the case of a penal measure is to produce a measurable change in behaviour of offenders in terms of reconviction statistics or some other measure of individual change. This report on community service is an evaluation of the former kind. To attempt an evaluation of community service on the basis of reconvictions or of unsatisfactory terminations of orders so soon would have been premature, because the knowledge that such an evaluation was to take place might have inhibited the use of community service orders with more serious offenders or in more imaginative work settings. Also the probation and after-care services in the experimental areas have gained expertise from their early experience. The figures for unsatisfactory termination following breach of an order are in any case likely to be misleading (see Chapter 4).

The lack of information about the long term effects of community service on offenders is inevitable at this stage of the scheme's development; but, even where long term evaluative research has been done on other forms of treatment, the typical conclusion reached has been that 'evidence supporting the efficacy of correctional treatment is slight, inconsistent and of questionable reliability'([5]). Thus, if it were to be argued that community service orders should not pass beyond the experimental stage until much more information has been gained, it would involve the application of standards to the scheme which many, if not all, extant penal treatments would fail to reach.

Rationale

In civil law, reparation to the appellant is the basic remedy. In criminal law, the victim is not always identifiable (if indeed there is a victim at all) and hence redress to the victim can never be a remedy universally applicable, though sections 1 to 5 of the Criminal Justice Act 1972* did extend provisions for compensation in criminal cases. However, offenders can make reparation to the community at large by working for it. On occasions, a sentence analogous to community service has been suggested, often in the context of reparation to the community in general. For example, Hauser[6] discussed in 1963 in the context of 'alternatives to the normal prison sentence', 'selective service' in which 'men involved would have to undertake work of social value, either full-time or on a part-time basis. This is based on the principles governing the treatment of conscientious objectors and underlines the compensation theory.' Cohen[7] quotes a suggestion made in 1964 that 'offences committed by "mods and rockers" should be punished by making the offenders work, which work should involve "visible restitution".' Del Vecchio[8], in 1969 developed the idea of offenders 'doing honest work under proper control' where harm from their offences was of concern to 'fellow members of the society, whence comes a need for reparation of a public nature, going beyond private compensation': the implication in Del Vecchio's paper is, however, that the reparation is in money earned from work rather than in work itself. Gibbens[9] in 1970 referred to the possibility that 'many offenders could only make compensation by providing their labour . . . this might involve them in difficulties which would make them almost prefer to go to prison': his remarks were in the context of restitution to individuals rather than to society generally.

Although possibly the most obvious aspect of community service is reparation to the community, as the Wootton Report remarks (paras. 33 and 34) such service 'should appeal to adherents of different varieties of penal philosophy. To some, it would simply be a more constructive and cheaper alternative to short sentences of imprisonment; by others it would be seen as introducing into the penal system a new dimension with an emphasis on reparation to the community; others again would regard it as a means of giving effect to the old adage that the punishment should fit the crime; while still others would stress the value of bringing offenders into close touch with those members of the community who are most in need of help and support. . . . These different approaches are by no means incompatible'.

Once community service is set up, it looks to the court for its clientele, and the court in turn looks to probation officers for recommendations about offenders' suitability to be ordered to do community service.

As probation officers may be expected to focus mainly on treatment, and sentencers often on punishment, the probation officer who organises community service has a difficult task; he has to develop not only a 'therapeutic' scheme which his probation officer colleagues can approve, but also one which sentencers will consider a realistic alternative to prison[10]. The problem was

---

* now ss.35 to 38. Powers of Criminal Courts Act 1973.

noted by the former Director of the Inner London Community Service Centre
([11]):

> 'because of its appeal to the widest range of penal philosophies, community
> service can appropriately be described, at least at this stage, as a vaguely
> determined project. . . . the experience thus far has shown that there is little
> harmony between the sentencers and those who have to implement community
> service orders. It seems essential to resolve these issues if the future of com-
> munity service is to be of use to courts and satisfying to the probation service'.

A different perspective on the same point is given by another community
service organiser, in Durham([10]):

> 'The community service order, therefore is something of a chameleon, which
> is able to merge into any penal philosophic background. Insofar as it deprives
> the offender of his spare time it can be seen as punitive; reparation (if not
> necessarily in kind) can be seen to be exacted; the community service order
> provides the offender with a setting in which he can make practical expressions
> of atonement; probation officers will readily identify the group therapy and
> "befriending" facets inherent in the community service tasks. It is this very
> versatility that provides the community service order with its greatest poten-
> tial. It may well be that confidence in the scheme among probation officers
> and sentencers [in this area] is now growing.'

Community service places the offender in the role of helper rather than helped.
The first question one community service organiser asks an offender who is
ordered to perform community service is 'What do you think you have got to
offer?' In another area, each offender who is being considered for a community
service order is given a leaflet with the following words in bold type: 'Community service helps you to help others. A challenge worth accepting?' One
could over-simplify by characterising the underlying question in much probation casework as 'What are your problems?' Community service, on the other
hand, is concerned with offenders' skills and strengths. Probation in emphasis
directs itself to remedying the problems and weaknesses of the offender. Some
probation officers may find the contrast between the approach to probation and
to community service a considerable change in emphasis. This may have been
exacerbated by the idea that community service is a tariff sentence rather than an
individualised sentence, so that 'sentence will be determined bearing some
relationship to the accused's culpability' rather than 'the needs of the accused'
(([12]), page 4). The view of community service as a tariff sentence was implicit in
earlier pronouncements in Inner London([13]) but does not accord with present
thinking and practice in that area. By contrast, in Nottingham, the community
service organiser suggested that the court should assess hours in terms of:

> '(a) The gravity of the offence and previous record of convictions, and such
> other matters as would normally be weighed in passing sentence.

(b) The capacity of the offender to take some regular responsibility for his attendance over an extended period.

(c) The extent of his work and domestic responsibilities and other pressures he may be facing'([14]).

CHAPTER 2

The Suitability of Offenders for Community Service

There are two aspects of this topic. First, what is the place of the community service sentence in the range of sentencing alternatives? Secondly, what personal characteristics or social circumstances are predictive of suitability for community service? Provisional views are given below.

The place of community service in the range of sentencing alternatives for imprisonable offences

When the Criminal Justice Act 1972 was before Parliament, Ministers made clear that the community service order was intended primarily as a method of dealing with persons who might otherwise be sentenced to short terms of imprisonment, and the Home Office continues to commend that aim. In three of the six experimental areas the Chief Probation Officers or working groups set up by them have tended to view community service as primarily or only an alternative to custody. In the other three areas community service is regarded as having a wider use, and in one of these the position is defended by the argument that, if community service were primarily an alternative to custody, the probation officer writing a social inquiry report must expect that the court would consider making a custodial sentence before he would be in a position to recommend the alternative of community service.

Types of offender suitable for community service

The Wootton Committee([2]) made no attempt to categorize precisely the types of offender for whom community service might be appropriate. They suggested, however, that, while inappropriate for trivial offences, it might well be suitable for some cases of theft, for unauthorized taking of vehicles, for some of the more serious traffic offences, and for some malicious damage or minor assault. They recommended that community service should not be confined to any particular age group, although the young offender was a likely candidate since many of the volunteers with whom he might be working would be teenagers. They considered that offenders of either sex might profit from working for the benefit of those in need, and mentioned in particular offenders suffering from domestic isolation.

The criteria of suitability for community service given by each of the six probation and after-care areas were as follows –

Durham([15])

Offenders must have 'personal and social circumstances such that probation is not necessary', and the circumstances should be such that the sentencers genuinely have it in mind to make a sentence of imprisonment. However 'in practice the community service client will not necessarily always be on the brink of a prison sentence'. The offenders must be willing consenters to participation in the scheme, rather than unwilling or 'ambivalent consenters'. Offences for which community service might be suitable: vandalism, dangerous driving, burglary, theft and assault. '. . . In the final analysis the matching of offender to project would be the most critical piece of a jigsaw in deciding upon suitability.'

The offender most suited to community service was described as follows in 1974[10] –

'He is of a fairly stable personality with a motivation towards community service at a level over and above that of token consent to the court viz he is genuinely stimulated at the prospect of performing community service; he more often than not is at a loose end in his spare time and . . . links onto an "unattached" group of equally non-involved associates (the gang); adverse social relationships produce adverse social behaviour, to the despair of his supportive parents who see his delinquency as alien to the family moral code; he has a good work record e.g. when at work he is punctual and a good attender; he is usually a person who has frequented the criminal courts and, for this reason, might be in jeopardy of losing his freedom; or he is someone who has experienced other methods of treatment, including custodial, but apparently to no avail. He steals'.

Inner London[13]

(a) 'It is hoped that community service orders will be made as an alternative to terms of imprisonment of up to 12 months.'

(b) 'The offender is expected to be in employment and of a settled address.'

(c) Personality: isolated, withdrawn; under-achieving; purposeless; those who have had little opportunity to contribute positively to society.

(d) Not suitable for violent offenders, drug users or alcoholics, the mentally ill or disturbed offender, sexual offenders.

(e) 'The validity of the experiment will best be tested by the widest selection of offenders nominated by individual probation officers using their own judgment.'

Kent[16]

Personality factors indicating suitability are:

(a) Purposelessness; persons who have little opportunity for making a positive contribution in society.

(b) Those who function below their potential and may be helped and encouraged by a working group situation.

(c) The isolated and withdrawn person who does not relate well in the case-work setting.

(d) 'The person who is at variance with a particular law rather than law breaking in general, whose offence might reflect certain attitudes towards society and be seen more as a community's problem than a psychological problem; e.g. cannabis smoking'.

(e) Those who may need to work out a sense of guilt.

Nottingham (in a letter of September 1972)

Not suitable:

(a) The psychotic or highly disturbed.

(b) The heavily addicted – to drugs or alcohol.

(c) Those who have committed a serious sexual offence.

(d) Those of very low intelligence.

(e) Those who lack social maturity or self-control.

(f) Unsuitable because of crisis situation in their lives.

Those for whom it would be particularly suitable:

(a) The isolated and withdrawn.

(b) Those lacking in social training who need an experience of consistency and continuity.

(c) Seriously disadvantaged people whose offences might be related to lack of opportunity at various stages in their lives.

(d) Those whose crimes may be serious but whose background is fairly stable.

(e) Actors-out – chip on shoulder, low self-esteem, purposeless livers who are always on the receiving end and believe the world owes them a living.

'. . . on a rough basis, community service would have most relevance to men and women between the ages of 17 and 30'.

South West Lancashire[17]

'The community service order . . . is a sentence in its own right and furthermore, is a constructive alternative to the imposition of "negative" sentences which may have little positive personal impact. It is now a practical working alternative to shorter custodial sentences . . .' but is considered inappropriate where –

(a) the protection of the community is an overriding consideration;

(b) professional casework support is needed;

(c) offenders are extremely aggressive, or are serious sexual deviants; firmly addicted to drugs or alcohol, or highly disturbed, or seriously mentally ill.

South West Lancashire was the only area in which women were excluded when the scheme started: they no longer are.

Shropshire

A sufficient diversity of tasks is available in Shropshire for a wide range of offenders. In 1972 the only category of exclusion mentioned was offenders 'requiring extensive casework'.

A content analysis of social inquiry reports

In mid-1973 the Research Unit did a content analysis of 519 social inquiry reports made in the six experimental areas in an attempt to discover if any specific characteristics of offenders were mentioned by probation officers when making a recommendation for, or considering, a community service order. These social inquiry reports were sent to the Research Unit from the probation areas and relate to cases in which, at some stage before sentence, community service had been considered. These included cases where a community service order had not been recommended by a probation officer, and cases where such a recommendation had or had not been taken up by the court.

After discussions with those involved in community service administration, and a preliminary examination of social inquiry reports, a content analysis form was produced, and modified so as to yield high inter-rater reliability*, and to include categories related to 18 main topics for investigation. These topics were: family background, marital or sexual environment, employment, intelligence, previous criminal record, finance, the possibility of a custodial sentence, the likely effect of a community service order, friends, leisure, involvement in voluntary work, drinking habits, home area, general reliability, education, military experience, and drug usage. Distribution of usage of the categories in each of the topics was calculated, to enable comparisons to be made between those recommended for community service and those considered but not recommended; between recommendations which were or were not taken up; and between the six experimental areas. No statistically reliable differences were found between these groups**. (For example, no one type of education was mentioned significantly more times in reports containing a community service recommendation that was acted on than in those where the recommendation was made but not acted on.) It was tempting to infer that there were no personal characteristics or social circumstances of offenders which probation officers used as general indicators of community service suitability. However, caution should be used in making that inference, since many social inquiry reports were silent on some of the topics mentioned above. Furthermore, all the social inquiry reports analysed were concerned with cases that were at some stage considered for community service.

---

* i.e. agreement between two people making judgements independently of each other on the classification of the material.

** 270 significance tests (chi square or Fisher Yates Exact test, as appropriate) were performed. The number of these yielding statistically significant results was sufficiently small to be attributed to chance, so they may be discounted.

Social inquiry reports and community service – The sentencing exercise

One possible reason for the inconclusive results of the content analysis was that it was carried out before probation officers had formed specific ideas about suitability for community service. In January 1974 (after community service had been in operation for 12 months) a further investigation was made. The method used to investigate the factors influencing a decision whether to recommend community service was an amended version of one developed by Carter, Chandler and Wilkins[18], [19] and [20]. A set of 24 index cards was printed with the name of a different topic normally dealt with in a social inquiry report (e.g. 'employment history'); on the reverse of the card was printed information relating to a specific case abstracted from a social inquiry report. Each probation officer was seen in his own office and asked to consider the topics and to choose, in order of importance, which cards to turn over so as to read the specific information on the back, with a view to considering whether a person was suitable for community service or not. He was then given a set of cards dealing with another case (i.e. cards with the same topics on one side but different information on the reverse) and asked to choose the topics with no particular sentence in mind. The order of the information-seeking in each case and the recommendation made were recorded by the researcher. (The information used in the exercise is presented as Appendix 1). A pilot survey of 15 probation officers was carried out in the Nottingham area. After minor adjustments, the technique was used on a sample of 55 probation officers in South West Lancashire (26 officers), Shropshire (14 officers) and Durham (15 officers). The officers were sampled on an office basis, 30 officers being selected from South West Lancashire and 15 each from Shropshire and Durham. The shortfall from 30 and 15 in the numbers presented above was a result of illness and unexpected court duty. It is intended to include London, Nottingham and Kent in this exercise at a later date.

In South West Lancashire the ages of officers interviewed ranged from 25 to 56 years (mean age 38), in Shropshire from 26 to 59 (mean age 40) and in Durham 23 to 52 (mean age 37). In South West Lancashire the years of experience ranged from 0·5 to 27 (mean 5·7 years), in Shropshire from 0·67 to 27 (mean 7 years) and in Durham from 0·75 to 16 years (mean 6·5 years). The results of this, the first part of the exercise, are shown in Tables 3 and 4.

In the second part of the exercise, each officer was asked to give some thought to those characteristics of offenders which excluded community service as a possible sentence, and to those characteristics which would encourage him to recommend community service. (This was because the first part of the exercise showed which characteristics were relevant, but not which aspects of those characteristics would lead to a recommendation for or against community service.) Each officer was given a list of the topics which had appeared on the front of the index cards, and was asked to write against those topics he thought relevant the aspects that inclined or disinclined him to recommend community service: he was given three weeks to complete this task and asked to return the

12

list in the stamped addressed envelope provided. The results, from South West Lancashire and Shropshire only, are shown in Table 6.

Two sample offenders were used in the exercise; one had successfully completed a community service order, and the other was considered by an experienced probation officer as a typical probationer. Some of the probation officers were asked to consider the community service case for community service, and the probation case with no particular sentence in mind. The others were asked to consider the community service case with no particular sentence in mind, and the probationer for community service. No officer was told until after the exercise what had been the original recommendation for either case.

Table 1

Recommendations by probation officers: 'Open' consideration

	Community service case	Probation case
South West Lancashire		
Community Service	6	1
Probation	5	11
Other	1	2
Shropshire		
Community Service	4	1
Probation	—	5
Other	2	2
Durham		
Community Service	2	1
Probation	2	5
Other	2	3

Table 2

Recommendations by probation officers: community service consideration

	Community service case	Probation case
South West Lancashire		
Community Service	12	4
Probation	1	8
Other	1	—
Shropshire		
Community Service	6	2
Probation	2	4
Other	—	—
Durham		
Community Service	8	4
Probation	1	2
Other	—	—

Table 1 shows, by area, the distribution of recommendations when the officers were asked to make a recommendation without bearing a specific sentence in mind. Table 2 shows the distribution when they were asked to consider community service specifically.

Looking at Table 1 and Table 2 together, 38 out of 55 officers recommended community service in the community service case used. Even where the probation officer dealt with the community service case without an instruction to consider community service, half of them (12 out of 24) nonetheless recommended community service. Thus, at least for the case chosen, there is some agreement between probation officers about suitability for community service. There is less agreement in recommending the community service case for community service than in recommending the probation case for probation, where 21 out of 31 officers recommended probation when given no instruction to consider community service, and 14 out of 24 in the presence of such an instruction.

The order in which, in the first part of the exercise, the topics were chosen by each probation officer in each area was recorded, and the mean rank of each topic was calculated. This was done for each area, and separately for each of the

Table 3

Mean ranking of topics by area

(a) *Considering community service*

South West Lancashire	Shropshire	Durham
Offence	Previous convictions	Offence
Previous convictions	Age	Personality
Age	Offence	Reaction to present offence
Personality	Personality	Employment history
Reaction to present offence	Family relationships	Previous convictions
Employment history	Employment history	Present employment
Medical history	Medical history	Medical history
Interests and activities	Reaction to previous sentences	Age
Reaction to previous sentences	Reaction to present offence	Family relationships
Marital situation	Present employment	Reaction to previous sentences
Present employment	Interests and activities	Interests and activities
Family relationships	Marital situation	Intelligence
Intelligence	Drugs	Marital situation
Family criminality	Father	Peers
Peers	Home	Father
Father	Family criminality	Home
Drugs	Appearance	Mother
Siblings	Mother	Family criminality
Mother	Peers	Education
Drink	Intelligence	Drugs
Home	Siblings	Drink
Education	Education	Siblings
Finance	Drink	Finance
Appearance	Finance	Appearance

two experimental conditions i.e. community service consideration and open consideration. The degree of agreement between probation officers in the order of their choice was calculated for each area by means of Kendall's coefficient of concordance. There was significant agreement between officers in each of the three areas ($p < \cdot 001$ in each case). Tables 3 and 4 show the mean order of choice of cards for each area for either kind of consideration. The agreement between mean rankings in the two types of consideration is high in all these areas ($p < \cdot 00003$ in each case, Kendall's tau).

Table 4

Mean ranking of topics by area

(b) *Open consideration*

South West Lancashire	Shropshire	Durham
Offence	Offence	Offence
Previous convictions	Previous convictions	Previous convictions
Age	Age	Family relationships
Marital situation	Personality	Personality
Personality	Family relationships	Age
Family relationships	Employment history	Reaction to present offence
Reaction to present offence	Marital situation	Employment history
Employment history	Present employment	Present employment
Mother	Reaction to present offence	Marital situation
Father	Reaction to previous	Father
Present employment	sentences	Mother
Interests and activities	Father	Interests and activities
Family criminality	Family criminality	Reaction to previous
Intelligence	Intelligence	sentences
Reaction to previous	Mother	Peers
sentences	Medical history	Home
Home	Interests and activities	Siblings
Education	Home	Medical history
Peers	Education	Intelligence
Medical history	Drink	Drink
Siblings	Peers	Education
Drink	Siblings	Family criminality
Drugs	Drugs	Drugs
Appearance	Finance	Finance
Finance	Appearance	Appearance

The inference from the results presented in Tables 3 and 4 is that probation officers use a similar information-seeking strategy when making any specific kind of information search, and that there is similarity of strategy between information searches when considering community service and when making an open consideration. The general similarity of approach however does not preclude the possibility that individual kinds of information are more relevant to officers in making one kind of decision than another. First it was decided to make individual comparisons of each of the 24 topics. Information was compared as between the two kinds of consideration by the Mann-Whitney U Test.

Those topics on which there was a difference (with a probability of ·1 or less, two-tailed test) are presented as Table 5.

Table 5

Topics differing in importance in community service and open consideration

	Topic	Probability
(a) *More important in community service consideration*		
South-west Lancashire	Drug usage	·0384
	Medical history	·0404
Shropshire	Interests and activities	·0366
	Medical history	·0602
Durham	Medical history	·0060
	Personality	·0614
(b) *More important in general consideration*		
South-west Lancashire	Offender's mother	·0644
Shropshire	Offence	·0258
Durham	Siblings	·0308
	Family relationships	·0332
	Previous convictions	·0990

At the end of the exercise each officer who had completed it was asked to give the reasons for his recommendations. For those who recommended community service for the community service case, the reasons given (if mentioned by more than one officer) are recorded below:

1. To keep offender out of prison	18
2. Good work record/good worker	15
3. Definite motive for offence	10
4. Plans to get married shortly	9
5. Has a pleasant personality	9
6. Seems to be changing his ways	7
7. Offence committed while in distress	9
8. No drink problem	5
9. Community service will widen his interest	5
10. Seems to understand his own problems	4
11. No drug problem	3
12. Medically fit	3
13. Probation not required	2

As earlier stated, each officer involved in the sentencing exercise was given three weeks in which to indicate, on a list of the topics on the front of the index cards, the factors for each topic which inclined or disinclined him to recommend community service. The response rate from South West Lancashire was 12 out of 26 (this includes a nil response from one office), and for Shropshire was seven out of 14 (one of those was completed incorrectly and had to be excluded). The contents of the 19 forms are recorded in Table 6. Results from the two areas are combined because the numbers involved are small.

It seems odd that, above and in Table 6, the criteria officers appear to use in making decisions about community service are not those to which they turned first in the exercise (see Tables 3 and 4). In fact, several judge the information to which they turned first as not important in making a decision about community service. It seems likely that officers regard certain information as essential background for their deliberations, whether or not they then consciously use it in reaching a decision. However it is tempting to feel that those who, for example, judge offence as irrelevant to a community service recommendation would have reported otherwise had one of the cases given to them involved a very serious offence. It is felt that this sort of information, chosen early, changes the range of alternatives within which officers consider it sensible to make a choice of recommendation.

Table 6

Factors favourable and unfavourable to a community service recommendation

	Factors favourable to a community service recommendation		Factors unfavourable to a community service recommendation	
Offence	Not important	8	Sex	9
	Burglary/Theft	5	Violence	7
	Taking and driving away	4	Not important	4
	Wilful/criminal damage	4	Drugs	2
	Any	3	Very trivial	2
	Minor assaults	1	Murder	2
	Drugs	1	Confidence tricks	1
			Drink	1
			Very serious	1
			Psychopathic nature	1
Previous convictions	Not important	13	Not important	9
	Any but sex and violence	2	History of violence	4
	History of petty offences	1	History of sex offences	3
	Few	1	Long criminal history	2
	Long break in convictions	1	Poor record of co-operation	2
			First offender	1
			Mental disorder	1
Age	Not important	9	Not important	12
	17+	2	30+	2
	19–29	1	Elderly	2
	17–45	1	17–19	1
	17–49	1	45+	1
	17–22	1	50+	1
			Senile	1

	Favourable		Unfavourable	
Reaction to present offence	Regretful	5	Not important	12
	Co-operative	5	Not guilty plea	6
	Accepts guilt	5	Need for casework	1
	Wants to improve	4	Unfeeling	1
	Not important	2	Indifferent	1
Present employment	Not important	14	Shift work	6
	Regular	1	Not important	5
	Stable	1	Lengthy hours	5
	Lazy	1	Unstable	1
	Unemployed at time of offence	1	Professional	1
			Community service could affect job	1
Employment history	Erratic	4	Not important	9
	Not important	3	Bad record	4
	Poor	3	People in sheltered work	4
	Good	2	History of idleness	1
	Irregular	1		
	Skilled	1		
Siblings	Not important	17	Not important	18
	Supportive	1		
Finance	Not important	17	Not important	15
	Reasonable	1	In debt	2
			Fine has never been tried	1
Peers	Not important	16	Not important	11
	Tendency to be led by peers	1	Peers a negative influence	4
	Change of peer group needed	1	Peers hostile to community service	1
			Peers anti-authority	1
			Peers already on community service	1
Medical history	Not important	10	Not important	10
	Good health	4	Disabled	6
	Fit	2	Mentally ill	5
	Good physique	1	Unfit	1
	Normal	1		
Marital situation	Not important	16	Not important	11
	Single	1	Matrimonial trouble	3
	Stable	1	Young children at home	3
			Infirm wife	1
Drugs	Not important	18	Addicted	11
			Not important	3
			Needs treatment	2
			Drug takers	2

	Favourable		Unfavourable	
Parents	Not important	17	Not important	18
	Parents should favour			
	community service	1		
Appearance	Not important	12	Not important	12
	Normal	6	Deformed	4
			Disfigured	4
			Wild-looking	1
			Dirty	1
Education	Not important	18	Not important	18
Intelligence	Not important	18	Not important	10
	Good average	1	Subnormal	6
	Average	1	Low I.Q.	2
	Below average	1		
Personality	Not important	12	Not important	8
	Withdrawn	2	Psychopathic	5
	Needs stimulation	1	Anti-authority	4
	Relates well	1	Paranoid	4
	Reasonable outlook	1	Immature	4
	No confidence	1	Violent	2
	Low ability	1	Aggressive	2
			Distressed	2
			Manipulative	1
			Unco-operative	1
			Withdrawn	1
			Maladjusted	1
			Casework needed	1
Family Criminality	Not important	18	Not important	18
Home	Not important	18	Not important	18
Interests and activities	Not important	10	Not important	17
	Few interests	6	Fully committed to	
	Interests similar to		constructive activities	1
	community service	2		
Family Relationships	Not important	18	Hostile wife	9
			Not important	6
			Poor	1
			Lack of understanding	1
			Probation needed	1
Drink	Not important	12	Alcoholic	12
	Recognises drink problem	4	Refuses to acknowledge	
	Where change of habits		problem	4
	could help	1	Drinks to excess	1
	Drinks because nothing else to do	1	Not important	1

CHAPTER 3

The Practice of Community Service

Recommendations made and sentences passed

The following information is derived from a research form filled in by probation officers when preparing social inquiry reports on offenders considered for community service. These are the cases where court, counsel or probation officer has mentioned the possibility of community service, or where the probation officer has independently considered community service before deciding not to recommend it.

Tables 7 to 13 present data on the relationship between probation officer recommendations and sentences passed in cases for which information was available in the Research Unit on 1st June 1974. Taking all experimental areas together, the court has acted on a probation officer's recommendation of community service in 853 cases out of 1158 (74%). Of the 1038 orders on which data are presented, 185 (18%) were made against the recommendation of the probation officer or where he expressed no opinion about community service. This figure can be compared with the 25% of probation orders made in two of the areas in the absence of a recommendation for probation (data gathered by the Research Unit, to be published).

Table 7

Community Service (CS) recommendations by probation officers (POs) and court disposals: Durham

Numbers in brackets are suspended sentences. They are included in the adjacent number

	CS order made		Other non-cus-todial disposal		Custodial disposal	
	PO recommends CS		PO recommends CS		PO recommends CS	
	Yes	No	Yes	No	Yes	No
Court specified CS consideration when asking for social inquiry report	22	5	—	—	3	—
PO recommends CS on his own initiative	45		14(4)		9	
Social inquiry report does not mention CS. Court asks PO in court for view on CS	—	4	—	—	—	—
No mention of CS before sentence		14				
Totals	67	23	14(4)	—	12	—

Table 8

Community Service (CS) Recommendations by probation officers (POs) and court disposals: Inner London

Numbers in brackets are suspended sentences. They are included in the adjacent number.

	CS order made		Other non-cus-todial disposal		Custodial disposal	
	PO recommends CS		PO recommends CS		PO recommends CS	
	Yes	No	Yes	No	Yes	No
Court specified CS consideration when asking for social inquiry report	146	28	6(1)	19(3)	2	3
PO recommends CS on his own initiative	162		12(9)		7	
Social inquiry report does not mention CS. Court asks PO in court for view on CS	2	5	—	4	1	—
No mention of CS before sentence		22				
Totals	310	55	18(10)	23(3)	10	3

Table 9

Community Service (CS) recommendations by probation officers (POs) and court disposals: Kent

Numbers in brackets are suspended sentences. They are included in the adjacent number.

	CS order made		Other non-cus-todial disposal		Custodial disposal	
	PO recommends CS		PO recommends CS		PO recommends CS	
	Yes	No	Yes	No	Yes	No
Court specified CS consideration when asking for social inquiry report	22	9	—	5	—	1
PO recommends CS on his own initiative	85		31(16)		24	
Social inquiry report does not mention CS. Court asks PO in court for view on CS	—	2	—	1(1)	—	1
No mention of CS before sentence		9				
Totals	107	20	31(16)	6(1)	24	2

Table 10

Community Service (CS) recommendations by probation officers (POs) and court disposals: Nottingham

Numbers in brackets are suspended sentences. They are included in the adjacent number.

	CS order made		Other non-cus-todial disposal		Custodial disposal	
	PO recommends CS		PO recommends CS		PO recommends CS	
	Yes	No	Yes	No	Yes	No
Court specified CS consideration when asking for social inquiry report	54	6	10(4)	7(1)	3	2
PO recommends CS on his own initiative	145		68(30)		54	
Social inquiry report does not mention CS. Court asks PO in court for view on CS	3	18	1(1)	5(3)	—	4
No mention of CS before sentence		18				
Totals	202	42	79(35)	12(4)	57	6

Table 11

Community Service (CS) recommendations by probation officers (POs) and court disposals: Shropshire

Numbers in brackets are suspended sentences. They are included in the adjacent number.

	CS order made		Other non-cus-todial disposal		Custodial disposal	
	PO recommends CS		PO recommends CS		PO recommends CS	
	Yes	No	Yes	No	Yes	No
Court specified CS consideration when asking for social inquiry report	6	—	2(1)	3	—	—
PO recommends CS on his own initiative	19		18(5)		6	
Social inquiry report does not mention CS. Court asks PO in court for view on CS	1	3	2(2)	2	—	—
No mention of CS before sentence		9				
Totals	26	12	22(8)	5	6	—

Table 12

Community Service (CS) recommendations by probation officers (POs) and court disposals: South-west Lancashire

Numbers in brackets are suspended sentences. They are included in the adjacent number.

	CS order made		Other non-custodial disposal		Custodial disposal	
	PO recommends CS		PO recommends CS		PO recommends CS	
	Yes	No	Yes	No	Yes	No
Court specified CS consideration when asking for social inquiry report	31	6	4	3	—	—
PO recommends CS on his own initiative	108		22(7)		4	
Social inquiry report does not mention CS. Court asks PO in court for view on CS	2	9	2	1	—	—
No mention of CS before sentence		18				
Totals	141	33	28(7)	4	4	—

Table 13

Community Service (CS) recommendations by probation officers (POs) and court disposals: All areas

Numbers in brackets are suspended sentences. They are included in the adjacent number.

	CS order made		Other non-custodial disposal		Custodial disposal	
	PO recommends CS		PO recommends CS		PO recommends CS	
	Yes	No	Yes	No	Yes	No
Court specified CS consideration when asking for social inquiry report	281	54	22(6)	37(4)	8	6
PO recommends CS on his own initiative	564		165(71)		104	
Social inquiry report does not mention CS. Court asks PO in court for view on CS	8	41	5(3)	13(4)	1	5
No mention of CS before sentence		90				
Totals	853	185	192(80)	50(8)	113	11

When a social inquiry report did not mention community service and the court subsequently asked the court duty probation officer for his view on community service suitability, the court did not accept this view in 47 out of 73 such cases (64%): in 41 of these 47 cases a community service order was made without a probation officer's recommendation. In addition to the low take-up rate of opinion in this situation, there were 90 cases where a community service sentence was passed though a probation officer had not recommended it, nor had there been discussion of it in court.

Table 14 summarises the take-up rate of probation officers' recommendations of community service, and shows the proportion of all orders made when a probation officer recommended against community service or made no recommendation about it.

Table 14

Relationship between probation officer's (PO) recommendation and sentence passed

Area	Percentage of PO recommendations for CS accepted	Percentage of all orders made where either PO made no recommendation or recommended against CS
Durham (93 recommendations)	72%	26%
Inner London (338 recommendations)	92%	15%
Kent (162 recommendations)	66%	16%
Nottingham (338 recommendations)	60%	17%
Shropshire (54 recommendations)	48%	32%
South-west Lancashire (173 recommendations)	82%	19%

Courts in Inner London are particularly high in their take-up rate of recommendations of community service. The take-up rate of recommendations is lowest in Shropshire, and in this county there is the highest proportion of community service orders made in the absence of a recommendation.

Table 15 presents data extracted from earlier tables, and shows that in all six areas, when a community service recommendation was not taken up, a custodial sentence having immediate effect was passed in only a minority of cases. This was so even in the areas (Inner London, Shropshire and Nottingham) where community service was regarded as primarily an alternative to custody. This does not in itself indicate that these courts used community service instead of non-custodial sentences.

Table 15

Disposal of cases where probation officer's (PO) recommendation of community service (CS) is not taken up

Area	Custodial sentence	Suspended sentence	Non-custodial sentence
Durham	12	4	10
Inner London	10	10	8
Kent	24	16	15
Nottingham	57	35	44
Shropshire	6	8	14
South-west Lancashire	4	7	21

Some clarifying information may be found in the disposal of those for whom the court takes the initiative in considering community service. Presumably when the court asks a probation officer to consider community service as a possible sentence when writing his social inquiry report, the sentence then passed, if not community service, will indicate something about how the court sees community service. Table 16 presents those cases where this happened. Although the numbers involved are very small, in all areas except Durham most such cases were not given custodial sentences having immediate effect. If all areas are combined, Table 16 shows that when a court initiated consideration

Table 16

Disposal of cases (excluding those given community service) where courts specified community service (CS) consideration when asking for a social inquiry report

	PO recommends CS			PO does not recommend CS		
	Immediate custody	Suspended imprisonment	Non-custodial sentence	Immediate custody	Suspended imprisonment	Non-custodial sentence
Durham	3	—	—	—	—	—
Inner London	2	1	5	3	3	16
Kent	—	—	—	1	—	5
Nottingham	3	4	6	2	1	6
Shropshire	—	1	1	—	—	3
South-west Lancashire	—	—	4	—	—	3
All areas	8	6	16	6	4	33

of community service and then did not make an order, a non-custodial sentence was passed instead, in the significant majority of cases.*

Taking the evidence together, then, it appears that sentencers in many cases seem to regard community service as an alternative to non-custodial sentences at least as much as, and possibly more than, an alternative to custodial sentences, and this finds support in the views of some probation officers (see pps. 52–57 for a fuller account of probation officer attitudes) where, it also finds support in the local research conducted in Durham[10] where in cases where a community service order was made, the probation officer who wrote the social inquiry report was asked, before the order was made, 'If an order is not made, do you think a custodial sentence – excluding a suspended sentence – would be probable possible or very unlikely?'. Of the 39 cases on which information is available, the officer said a custodial sentence was probable in 19 cases, only possible in 13 and very unlikely in 7.

This report does not attempt to estimate the number of people who may have been kept (albeit some only temporarily) from custodial sentences during the first 18 months of the experiment.

Numbers of orders made and type of court

The number of orders made in each area up to 30 June 1974, and the number of active orders at that date are shown in Table 17.

The figures in Table 17 give no indication of the rate of each area's development in relation to the size of its population. To provide a rough adjustment for

Table 17

Number of those made the subject of community service orders and number of orders active on 30 June 1974

Area	Total orders*	Active orders
Durham	99	49
Inner London	405	184
Kent	172	104
Nottingham	263	167
Shropshire	67	36
South-west Lancashire	186	141
All areas	1192	681

*Two orders made for one person at separate court appearances are both counted.

* A sign test shows significantly more non-custodial sentences to have been made in this situation, $z = 2\cdot81$, $p = \cdot005$, two-tailed test. Suspended sentences are included as custodial sentences. Other conventions about treating suspended sentences would increase the statistical significance of the result.

difference in the sizes of the probation and after-care areas involved, calculations were made of the number of community service orders made monthly in each area (a) per officer authorised to write social inquiry reports including a recommendation about community service, and (b) per social inquiry report written per month for adult courts. Table 18 presents both comparisons.

Table 18

Rates at which community service orders are made in the experimental areas relative to number of probation officers and to number of social inquiry reports written

Area	Index of Development 1	Index of Development 2
Durham	0·045	·046
Inner London	0·057	·016
Kent	0·180	·042
Nottingham	0·167	·041
Shropshire	0·087	·074
South-west Lancashire	0·087	·019

Index of Development 1 = $\dfrac{\text{Number of orders made per month}}{\text{Number of probation officers in areas which operate community service.}}$

Index of Development 2 = $\dfrac{\text{Number of orders made per month}}{\text{Number of social inquiry reports written per month on adults.}}$

The ordering of the areas according to the size of the index should not be taken too literally, since there are reasons (relating to the timing of the expansion within areas) why the comparisons favour some areas. The point of Table 18 is to show that the smaller schemes are in reality not under-developed relative to the larger ones.

Table 19 shows, for each area, the number of orders made by length and type of court. There are wide differences between individual courts. The proportion of longer orders (200 hours plus) varies from 0 to 56% between courts. If orders are divided into those of 150 hours or above and those below 150 hours, a significantly higher proportion of the longer orders is made in Crown Courts than in magistrates' courts in Durham, Inner London and Kent. A significantly lower proportion of long orders was made by Crown Courts in South West Lancashire.*

Table 20 shows the distribution by age and sex of those made the subject of community service orders, up to 30 June 1974. As will be seen, offenders on

---

* Durham, $\chi^2 = 6·40$, p < ·02; Inner London $\chi^2 = 4·41$, p < ·05; Kent $\chi^2 = 14·80$, p < ·001; South-west Lancashire $\chi^2 = 8·52$, p < ·01.

Table 19

Community service orders made by type of court and length of order

	Inner London		South-west Lancashire		Durham		Kent		Shropshire		Nottinghamshire		All areas	
	Higher Courts	Magistrates Courts	Crown Courts	Magistrates Courts	Crown Courts	Magistrates Courts	Crown Courts	Magistrates Courts	Crown Courts	Magistrates Courts	Crown Courts	Magistrates Courts	Crown Courts	Magistrates Courts
40 to 99 hrs	10	41	10	2	2	6	5	14	—	6	7	32	34	101
100 to 149 hrs	31	160	15	59	14	38	11	60	1	14	43	100	115	431
150 to 199 hrs	12	25	3	17	6	13	4	9	—	6	5	20	30	90
200+ hrs	8	26	2	35	7	4	15	9	1	5	12	25	45	104

Note. Orders are included from information available to the Research Unit on 1 June 1974. If orders are made to run consecutively, the aggregate hours are recorded as for one order.

Table 20

Age and sex of those made the subject of community service orders up to 30 June 1974

Age	Durham		Inner London		Kent		Nottingham		Shropshire		South-west Lancashire		All areas	
	Male	Female	Male	Female	Male	Female	Male	Female	Male	Female	Male	Female	Male	Female
17 to 20	63	3	209	5	82	—	114	10	36	—	106	—	610	18
21 to 24	17	2	101	4	39	2	63	5	13	1	33	—	266	14
25 to 28	8	—	37	3	21	—	27	3	5	—	23	—	121	6
29 to 32	—	1	12	1	3	—	13	3	6	—	9	—	43	5
33 to 36	1	—	12	1	5	1	10	—	3	—	8	—	39	2
37+	3	1	15	—	4	1	14	1	3	—	6	—	45	3

Table 21

Number of community service orders made each month since schemes commenced

	1973												1974				
	Jan	Feb	Mar	Apr	May	June	July	Aug	Sept	Oct	Nov	Dec	Jan	Feb	Mar	Apr	May
Durham	—	—	1	1	10	0	7	5	11	4	1	2	7	11	17	6	9
Inner London	25	36	18	18	16	10	16	12	5	26	25	9	29	47	32	24	29
Kent	—	—	—	1	8	2	3	7	3	9	11	6*	15	14	15	15	20
Nottinghamshire	9	15	9	7	11	13	10	11	6	9*	15	16	30	22	15	21	21
Shropshire	0	3	2	1*	4	3	13	1	0	3	1	2	5	3*	10	7	5
South-west Lancashire	—	5	6	3*	6	3	1	7	10	9	19	16	20	9	12	22	13
All areas	34	59	36	31*	55	31	50	43	35	60*	72	51*	106	106*	101	95	97

* Additional courts were empowered to make orders.

community service are drawn primarily from younger age groups, and at least one community service organiser has been concerned lest community service may come to be seen as exclusively a young man's punishment.

Table 21 shows changes in rate at which orders have been made for each area. Figure 1 shows this for all areas combined. The progress is erratic in some areas. This causes considerable difficulty for community service organisers, since work commitments must be geared to predicted (and in the event unpredictable) numbers. Rates seem sensitive to local difficulties and lack of publicity. In addition, numbers of recommendations of community service, the take-up of these recommendations by the court, and the frequency with which the court itself initiates consideration of community service may all be relevant. These are presented graphically for all areas combined (Figures 2 to 4).

Table 22 shows that the fluctuations in rate of making community service orders has been contributed to more by changes in number of probation officers' recommendations than by changes in numbers of court initiations. This implies that changes in the rate of orders may be influenced by changing views of probation officers rather than of sentencers. This may be an over-simplification however; for example, given a wide difference in usage between courts, it may be that probation officers restrict community service recommendations when they find the court unresponsive to them.

Table 22

Correlation between rate of community service orders and rate of recommendations independently of number of court initiations, and between rate of orders and number of court initiations independently of recommendations

	Correlation between recommendations and orders independently of court initiations	Correlation between orders and court initiations independently of recommendations
Durham	+ ·82	+ ·38
Inner London	+ ·90	+ ·41
Kent	+ ·87	+ ·46
Nottingham	+ ·87	+ ·63
Shropshire	+ ·71	+ ·38
South-west Lancashire	+ ·85	+ ·29

These figures are calculated by correlating number of orders per month with the number of recommendations per month, independently of the number of court specifications per month; and by correlating the number of orders per month with the number of court specifications, independently of the number of recommendations.

31

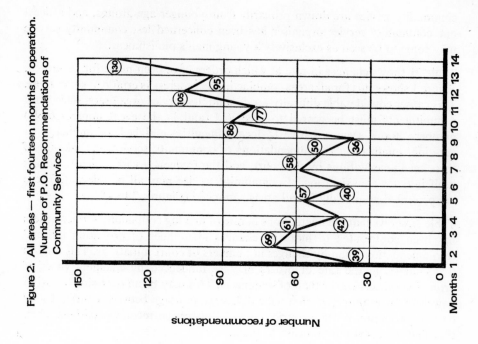

Figure 2. All areas — first fourteen months of operation. Number of P.O. Recommendations of Community Service.

Figure 1. Community Service Orders made per month in all areas combined.

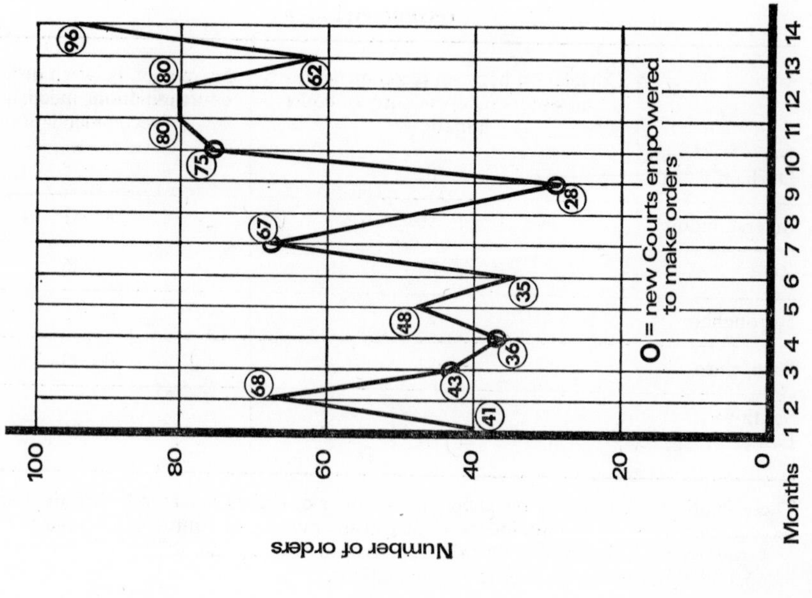

O = new Courts empowered to make orders

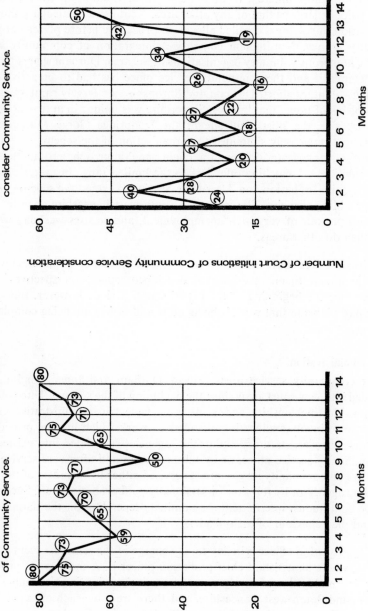

Figure 3. All areas — first fourteen months of operation. Percentage acceptance of P.O. recommendations of Community Service.

Figure 4. All areas — first fourteen months of operation. Number of cases in which Court asked P.O. to consider Community Service.

N.B.
The horizontal axis represents the first fourteen months of operation of each scheme irrespective of the month when they commenced.

33

Area differences in the practice of community service

Irrespective of its view of the place of community service in the range of sentences, each of the experimental areas has, by circumstances and emphasis, brought something different to the scheme. Inner London operates on a scale nearly twice as large as that of any other area. Kent has a particular philosophy of operation, involving a detailed allocation procedure before placement with a voluntary agency. Nottingham emphasises integration of community service with the numerous voluntary organisations in the area. Durham shares Nottingham's emphasis and the community service office has had to be active in stimulating voluntary effort. Durham and Shropshire are largely rural areas, with the problems of travel that implies. Shropshire was unique in at first using only one work site, the Blists Hill site of the Ironbridge Gorge Museum. This arrangement immensely simplified the organisation of the scheme but brought with it disadvantages (criticisms of a 'chain gang' approach, and limitations of the possibilities of matching offenders to the limited range of tasks) which led the Shropshire Probation and After-Care Service to extend the scheme to other work-providing agencies. The scheme in South-west Lancashire operates in an area with pockets of very high unemployment, and so uses weekday working more than do other areas.

Thus, because areas have different local pressures and different policies by which to accommodate them, they have all developed separate perspectives on the scheme since the beginning of the experimental period: however, the scheme has proved viable in that work is being done and orders are being completed in all areas.

Local administration

All six community service areas, except Durham and Inner London, have expanded into new court areas since the beginning of the scheme. Three of them, Durham, Nottinghamshire and Kent, now have two administrative centres. Each scheme involves allocating offenders to work which may be provided by voluntary agencies, statutory authorities, agencies stimulated into existence by the community service office, or by the probation and after-care service itself. Offenders on community service are supervised either by members of the work-providing agency or by full-time or sessionally-paid probation staff. Supervision may be continuous, intermittent, or nominal, depending on the nature of the task and the behaviour of the offender.

A senior probation officer is in day-to-day charge of the scheme, except in Inner London, where an assistant chief probation officer is. A main grade probation officer is employed exclusively on community service in Nottinghamshire, Durham and South-west Lancashire, and there are three such officers in Inner London. All areas employ full-time ancillaries: and in South-west Lancashire there is an administrative officer, in Inner London there is an executive officer and in Kent a senior ancillary. The role of the full-time ancillary differs as

34

between areas. For example in South-west Lancashire they are designated 'community service supervisors'. As the name implies, they do much supervision. In some other areas, for example Inner London, full-time ancillaries do no supervision. Areas appoint sessional task supervisors; in mid-1974, the number ranged from 20 in Inner London to one in South-west Lancashire. Community service organisers are agreed that ancillaries and sessional task supervisors are lynch-pins of the scheme.

The community service organiser in each area is involved in locating tasks, matching and allocating of offenders to tasks, liaising with work-providing agencies, sentencers and probation officers, following up 'difficult' offenders and initiating breach proceedings. (The organiser in Inner London is more a general administrator than is the case elsewhere.) Main grade probation officers are involved in similar kinds of work; those in Durham and Nottingham seem particularly active in finding new community service tasks. The ancillaries are concerned in liaison with work-providing agencies, general oversight of work schemes and supervision of offenders.

In all areas, except Durham and Shropshire, local probation officers are advised to contact the community service office before recommending community service to the court. In all areas careful matching of an offender to an available task is made before the first work allocation. The offender's experience in that first work task confirms, or otherwise, his suitability for that type of work: if he is unsuitable other work placements are tried. As a general rule, in Nottingham, Inner London and South-west Lancashire, an offender remains in one (suitable) allocation throughout his order, if the work continues to be available and he responds well. In Durham the policy is for varied work placements, while in Shropshire the issue remains undecided until the expansion of work opportunities allows more flexibility of allocation. The system in Kent deserves special mention: each offender is attached for at least eight hours to a small 'mobile task force' operated by the community service office, where he is assessed for future work. From there he is allocated to a semi-supervised work situation and then to a minimally supervised work situation depending on his performance; he may be transferred from one type of work to another, as his behaviour determines.

The community service offices' contact with offenders on community service is maintained through supervisors: the community service organisers themselves do not often see the offender after the induction interview and initial matching, unless, for example, the offender requires help of a personal nature, or breach proceedings are being contemplated. In Durham the community service organiser interviews each offender at least once, midway through the order, concerning his responses and attitudes to the scheme. The community service officer in Shropshire often sees offenders on community service during her regular visits to each work site. (The expansion of the scheme in Shropshire may restrict such visits in the future.)

35

The community service organiser in every area is careful to maintain contact with all groups in the community who are or may become interested in the community service scheme. In all areas he has had at least some contact with press, radio and television, either through formal press releases or more informally.

The operation of community service

Once a community service order is made, one of the community service staff interviews the offender and, in consultation with colleagues, decides then or later on a work placement. The time taken from the making of an order to an offender's first contact with the community service office is shown in Table 23. Data are for orders made in January and February 1974.

Table 23

Time in days from court appearance at which a community service order is made to first contact with representative of the probation and after-care service (orders made January and February 1974)

	Median days* to first contact	Interquartile range* of time in days to first contact
Durham	12	7·5
Inner London	4	2·5
Kent	4·5	5
Nottingham	10	11
Shropshire	14	—**
South-west Lancashire	5·5	5

* The median is the middle item in a series of numbers arranged in increasing order, e.g. the series of numbers 3, 4, 4, 5, 5, 6, 6, 7, the median is 5. The interquartile range is the difference between the 25% and 75% points in the series, counting in the same way (in this case the difference between 4 and 6, i.e. 2).

** Too few cases to be meaningful.

Table 24 shows the percentage of work appointments attended at which offenders came into contact with non-offenders. Given that even when there is an offender-only work group those on it can still come into contact with beneficiaries of service, the more usual work situation is one in which the offender has contact with non-offenders, whether beneficiaries of service or volunteers working with them.

These data are in principle, important, in that the Wootton Report[2] laid emphasis on the benefits to be gained by such contact. However, it appears that on at least some occasions supervisors were unclear about how, for example, to define a beneficiary. These data must therefore be treated with some caution.

In Appendix II are listed types of work performed on the community service scheme in each area up to 30 June 1974. There is a great diversity of tasks in all areas.

Table 24

Percentage of work appointments involving contact with beneficiaries and percentage of offender-only work groups

	Percentage of work appointments where there was contact with beneficiaries			Percentage of work appointments where there were offender-only work groups		
	July-Sept. 1973	Oct.-Dec. 1973	Jan.-Feb. 1974	July-Sept. 1973	Oct.-Dec. 1973	Jan.-Feb. 1974
Durham	84	98	92	1	0	2
Inner London	72	68	80	13	49	45
Kent	58	15	16	52	44	32
Nottingham	41	62	69	48	4	17
Shropshire	0	0	16	25	68	48
South-west Lancashire	61	59	78	19	14	2
Average All areas	53	50	58	26	30	24

Table 25

Percentage of hours worked during the year March 1973 to March 1974 on weekdays and weekends (Saturday and Sunday)

	Weekday	Weekend
Durham	31	69
Inner London	12	88
Kent	22	78
Nottingham	42	58
Shropshire	12	88
South-west Lancashire	65	35
Average all Areas	31	69

Table 25 presents the proportion of weekday and weekend working for each area during the year March 1973 to March 1974. It will be seen that South-west Lancashire has the highest proportion of weekday working by a substantial amount. Of the other areas, only Nottingham has a high proportion of weekday work.

Table 26 shows the average number of hours worked during February 1974 in each area by those on active community service orders (excluding orders made in February, and orders not worked at all during February or ending in that month). It will be seen that Durham has the highest average number of hours worked and South-west Lancashire the lowest. Given the distribution of lengths of orders in South-west Lancashire, such an average would lead to serious

37

Table 26

Mean and standard deviation of number of hours per offender worked on community service in each area. February 1974

	Mean in hours	Standard deviation in hours
Durham	21·25	12·59
Inner London	14·88	8·12
Kent	18·20	8·72
Nottingham	14·75	10·95
Shropshire	14·25	12·38
South-west Lancashire	9·86	7·13

N.B. This excludes orders on which no work was performed during February and orders which started or terminated during that month.

problems in completing within a year the orders made. This may well have been a rather bad month to choose for South-west Lancashire, since it coincided with a period of illness for the senior probation officer responsible for the scheme in South-west Lancashire.

While task supervisors have a crucial role in community service, and its success or failure may depend on them, a few occasions of extravagant crediting, by supervisors without the knowledge of probation officers, came to notice (even to an extent that, in effect, subverted the order of the court). This problem occurred in a few cases where the supervisor was paid sessionally by the probation and after-care authority and in others where the supervisor was employed by the work-providing agency. Probation officers administering the scheme quickly came to grips with the problem.

Figure 5 shows the average time in months taken to complete orders of various lengths made between January and June 1973 (all areas are combined). It will be seen that orders of 200 hours or over take on average 10 to 12 months to perform and this tends to support the majority view of community service organisers in the experimental areas that the maximum length of order (240 hours) is too long.

Table 27 presents the proportion of unsatisfactory failures to attend for work during the period January to February 1974 in each of the six areas. Some of the differences between areas may be due to different views as to what is 'unsatisfactory' held by the officers who classified failures to attend.

Weather data, from weather centres at London, Manchester, Watnall and Newcastle-upon-Tyne, were examined for each weekend between March 1973 and March 1974 so as to correlate rainfall and absenteeism for each of the areas, Inner London, South-west Lancashire, Nottingham and Durham. (Absenteeism was based on the proportion of non-attenders to total number of

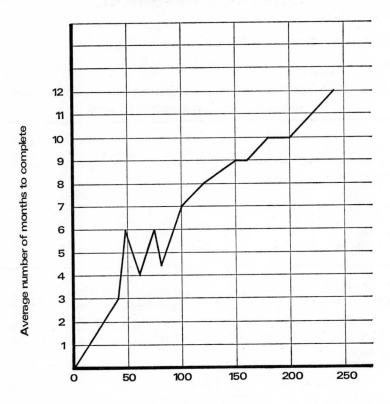

Figure 5. Time taken in months to complete
Community Service Orders of varying
lengths (all areas).

Table 27

**Percentage of unsatisfactory failures to attend for community service
work, January to February 1974**

Durham	4
Inner London	19
Kent	9
Nottingham	8
Shropshire	18
South-west Lancashire	6
Average all areas	11

N.B. The figure is a percentage of all appointments made, not all appointments attended.

offenders instructed to attend for work.) In no case was the relationship statistically significant (Inner London $r = -\cdot19$, Nottingham $r = +\cdot15$, South-west

Lancashire r = + ·12, Durham r = + ·13). Calculating the correlation for each quarter separately yielded no more statistically significant correlations than one would expect by chance. Rainfall thus does not appear to affect the extent of absenteeism.

Criminal record of those on community service

Table 28

Length of criminal records of offenders made subject to community service orders in each of the experimental areas

	Median number of previous convictions	Interquartile range of number of previous convictions
Durham (n = 81)	3	5
Inner London (n = 225)	4	5
Kent (n = 110)	3	5
Nottingham (n = 205)	4	10
Shropshire (n = 35)	3	6
South-west Lancashire (n = 101)	4	6

Table 28 presents the average (median) number of previous convictions of offenders made subject to community service orders in each area, and the spread (interquartile range) of number of previous convictions. It will be seen that the Inner London, Nottingham and South-west Lancashire offenders had the longer previous criminal records.

Table 29

Number of those given community service orders in each area by previous custodial experience

	Number of custodial sentences served			
	0	1	2-4	5+
Durham (n = 81)	49	20	9	3
Inner London (n = 225)	142	43	30	10
Kent (n = 110)	68	21	15	6
Nottingham (n = 205)	103	47	41	14
Shropshire (n = 35)	20	9	5	1
South-west Lancashire (n = 101)	53	19	20	9
All areas (n = 757)	435	159	120	43

Table 29 presents the number of those in respect of whom community service orders have been made and whose criminal records are available, and the extent of their previous custodial experience (excluding approved school). The proportion of those with custodial experience in the six areas is remarkably similar;

40

in Durham 40%, Inner London 37%, Kent 38%, Nottingham 50%, Shropshire 43% and South-west Lancashire 48%.

Table 30 specifies the nature of offences*, in respect of which community service orders were made in each area, where the offender's criminal record is available. Table 31 specifies by area the most common type of previous offence* of those offenders made subject to community service orders whose criminal records are available. As is to be expected, the bulk of offenders are typically convicted of property offences.

---

* The classification of offences is as follows:
   Offences against person – Assault, (including occasioning bodily harm, and indecent assault), unlawful sexual intercourse, etc.
   Property offences – Theft, robbery, burglary, criminal damage, handling stolen goods etc.
   Motoring offences – Drunk whilst driving, no licence, insurance etc. Driving while disqualified, dangerous driving etc, take and drive away.
   Miscellaneous – Including drug offences, forgery, possession of firearms.
   When there were equal numbers of previous offences in two or more categories, the offender was classified in the higher category (as they are listed above) of those in which his offences fell. This is because the categories of offence are judged to be broadly in order of decreasing seriousness.

41

Table 30

Types of offences for which community service orders were made in each area

	Durham (n = 81)	Inner London (n = 225)	Kent (n = 110)	Nottingham (n = 205)	Shropshire (n = 35)	South-west Lancashire (n = 101)	All areas (n = 757)
Offences against person	13	29	3	32	5	7	89
Property offences	40	100	66	100	19	55	380
Motoring offences	22	61	23	41	6	29	182
Miscellaneous	6	35	18	32	5	10	106

Table 31

Most common type of previous offence of those made subject to community service orders in each area

	Durham (n = 81)*	Inner London (n = 225)*	Kent (n = 110)*	Nottingham (n = 205)*	Shropshire (n = 35)*	South-west Lancashire (n = 101*)	All areas (n = 757)
Offences against person	7	13	10	24	3	1	58
Property offences	56	138	65	125	21	80	485
Motoring offences	5	35	10	29	3	15	97
Miscellaneous	1	18	10	11	6	1	47

* Numbers in a column do not add to the number at its head, because some offenders had no criminal record.

CHAPTER 4

Success and Failure on Community Service

The community service order is extant (though it may be inactive) until revoked, or discharged on completion. There are various problems involved in attempting to classify some community service orders in this way. For example, in a minority of cases, the supervising probation officer has treated an order as completed though all the hours ordered have not been worked: this has been arrived at by adding travelling time to the hours worked by an offender who has failed to keep appointments after working the bulk of his hours. In other cases, though most hours to be worked are still outstanding, the 12 months (or more) for completing them has passed; so the order has been considered terminated without an application to the court. It is probably best to regard these instances as expedients in the face of teething troubles of the scheme and overwork. None of the probation officers concerned would wish these instances to serve as a precedent and would no longer practice them themselves.

It is apparent that breach proceedings are not instigated in the same circumstances or at the same stage in all areas. Early on the community service organisers inclined to the view that breach proceedings should not be taken until there had been at least three failures (without reasonable excuse) to attend work appointments, but there are differing criteria about what is an acceptable absence, between the areas and between different stages of an order in any specific area. In two areas some clients (mainly those on shift work) are asked either to turn up for work whenever they can or to make their own arrangements with the agency to which they have been allocated. It is obviously difficult to assess an offender's community service work record in such a situation.

If a custodial sentence was passed for a further offence committed whilst the community service order was active, in some cases no action was taken where the time in which the order had to be completed would expire before the offender was released. The areas differ in their policy regarding cases where a custodial sentence would be completed before the end of the community service year. In one area the order was revoked; in another the order was held in abeyance during the period of custody; in yet another the offender was given the option of working on community service upon release (with or without application for an extension of the year).

There are other types of 'inoperative' active order. Some offenders go to live or work outside the experimental area, on a temporary or permanent basis. Although in theory they are available for community service work because no action has been taken regarding the order (usually because the offender may come back to the experimental area), in practice they do not work. Other offenders are unavailable because of sickness, or because of their regular employment (especially if working long hours to pay off debts or fines).

Considerations such as those above make enforcing and court action on a community service order a more complicated matter than may appear on the surface.

Success on Community Service

The success or otherwise of community service, as of any other penal measure, is assessed by change in behaviour of the offender. From experience, members of the Research Unit are convinced of the fact that much community service work is regarded as a positive experience by those on community service (see pages 58–59). The Research Unit asked each of the six experimental areas to nominate up to five completed cases as its successes. Two cases in each area (the first two on each area's list) are summarised below.

Cases nominated as successes, or 'cases which have given us satisfaction', by those who administer the community service scheme

Area 1

CASE 1. carried out his first work arrangement on 18.4.73. and his last on 25.5.73. During this time he kept all his 17 appointments.

All his work appointments were carried out at a charity's day centre. His duties included furniture renovation, ground clearance, gardening, fencing repairs and general maintenance, inside and outside the premises.

He worked well with little or no supervision and got on very well with the centre's staff and with the young children. As they arrived in the mornings he would assist the nurses in unstrapping and carrying them in from the ambulance and settling them down in the cleansing and changing room. The children are all incontinent but this did not deter him.

He was a reliable and consistent worker who had a very willing attitude and gave no trouble at all throughout the term of the order. He gives the impression that he has gained some confidence during his service and it is hoped that he will make renewed efforts at breaking his regrettably long spell of unemployment.

CASE 2. is a single man and the third of ten children. He lives with his parents and family in a highly delinquent quarter. Most of the family have been in conflict with the law and several have experienced all the forms of treatment available to the courts.

Following an elementary education and attendance at a special school for educationally subnormal children, where his achievements were limited, he was committed to an approved school: he absconded persistently and was transferred to a closed psychiatric hospital where he was detained for two years. Upon discharge, he committed offences which landed him in borstal and eventually in prison.

With 32 previous convictions, several years in institutions, a poor work record and the handicap of epilepsy, it was felt that he could only be accommodated in the community service workshop under fairly close supervision. He made an

45

excellent job of painting a boat owned by the probation and after-care service for use in connection with adventure training weekends; undertook the simple repair of toys damaged by handicapped children and worked very well in tidying up the workshop after building operations.

As he responded well to sympathetic handling and appreciated the opportunity to do something useful and worthwhile, he was placed with a charitable organisation that catered for handicapped children where he helped operate a Rotaprint machine and prepared literature for distribution to the general public. Occasionally he failed to keep work appointments, but regard was had to his limitations and his programme varied accordingly.

He was thus helped to realise a better potential. Had he been fined, he would have been unable to pay or at least taken a very long time to do so and would probably have preferred a relatively short spell in prison in default. It is thought that a counselling service such as would have been afforded him on probation would not have benefited him a great deal, and deprivation of liberty could have damaged him even further.

Area 2

CASE 1. As he could not be seen in the first few days of his order, a letter was sent suggesting he made his own way to the site and giving him full instructions about attendance and community service.

From 24 March 1973 until 30 April 1973, when he completed his 60 hours community service work, he worked hard and showed interest and maturity in community service.

While under the community service order, he became redundant in his employment. His community service had been so impressive that the place where he did it offered him a full-time labouring job; he accepted and began this work on 1 May 1973, after making considerable efforts to finish his community service beforehand.

This job was fairly short-lived and he left, with a good record, for other employment. He seems not to have been in trouble since completing his community service order.

CASE 2. From the start of his community service order he, and his co-defendant, were positive in their outlook on community service. His attendance throughout was good and he had a responsible attitude to attending regularly and maintaining continuity.

Between May and November 1973 he did the 160 hours work, partly during his summer holidays. He was always pleasant, friendly and enthusiastic to help in all ways. His concern for the well-being of others was apparent. If he had a problem he would talk about it. On most occasions he brought his girl friend, who worked quite enthusiastically as a volunteer. In her opinion he changed

46

during the course of his community service order, seemed to settle down more and was not so worried about his personal problems. She felt it was the best thing that could have happened to him. On the day the order was completed, he worked on for a brief period to the end of the day, and it was thought that, had his home been nearer, he would have continued with community service as a volunteer. There was no concern that he would become involved in any further offences during the course of his community service order, and he has not come to the notice of the court since it ended.

Area 3

CASE 1. was ordered 100 hours concurrently for offences of taking and driving away in October 1973. He was a young man of good education living away from home, who had dropped out and was living in a squat: when interviewed, he was able to talk about his drifting. He was placed in a youth club where he worked steadily for three evenings a week and on Sunday mornings, completing the order within two months. He was in touch soon after and had returned to his parents. He has a more purposeful way of life and community service may be said to have re-established him in society.

CASE 2. was ordered in June 1973 to do 150 hours community service for conspiracy and arson. A young man well known to the probation service and with problems associated with a brittle bone structure and small stature, he had had a series of disastrous personal relationships and was subject to violent emotional swings. He worked the whole of his 150 hours within the community where he lived. He had a wide variety of tasks ranging from personal services for the elderly to helping out with the young and, in addition, organised leaflet distribution, etc. He did a considerable amount of work of a similar nature which was not credited as statutory community service because of his feelings.

His order was fully completed in seven months. He caused no problems. He enjoyed what he was doing, put more into it than was asked of him, and was a real value to his own community.

Area 4

CASE 1. His work on the outings for old people on Saturdays and Sundays throughout the summer and the autumn did credit to the scheme and to this man. His initiative, kindness and willingness at every aspect of the Group impressed the organisers, the beneficiaries and the general public. He represented the best aspects of community service. Introduced by his supervising officer, he was interviewed by *The Observer* and the *Evening Post* and his work was filmed for BBC 'Man Alive'. His wife is also a valued member of the Group and they bring their child with them. They also managed to link up a 13-year-old probationer who had expressed interest in community service. Just before Christmas the Group held a small party and gave presents to him and his wife in recognition of their efforts.

47

Half way through the order he tore up his record card and said he wasn't interested in the formality of the order itself, he would come along willingly any time. After the order ended he put in for a house transfer to be nearer the Group. (His work with the Group has caused one influential councillor to change his mind about community service by offenders and to admit in public at an annual general meeting of the Group that he had judged the scheme too hastily.) Despite all the publicity that he has received, he remained unruffled and co-operative throughout. There was a major crisis about a third of the way through the order when he was charged with motoring offences committed some two years earlier. He was fined £95 but retained his licence.

CASE 2. completed community service very satisfactorily. Most of her 200 hours were spent with a voluntary organisation. She performed a number of tasks such as painting and decorating, gardening, clerical work, running a shop. She gained great support from the interest and concern which the organisation show for all those involved with them and it was an ideal placement. The supervisor even attempted to sort out her employment difficulties and arranged interviews for her with local colleges of education and the Department of Employment. She in turn acknowledged her attachment to her supervisor and the more she became invested in the organisation the more satisfaction she obtained. There were no adverse reports about her, and the only complaint was that she over-taxed herself in terms of physical effort. She is frail and prone to colds and chest complaints, and she does not eat properly or dress warmly enough.

She also attended a local luncheon club on ten occasions, helping to prepare and serve meals for old aged pensioners. Again progress was satisfactory though she never felt the same sense of involvement as with the first organisation, for which she would like to continue to work. Its chief value has been that she has begun to believe in herself again and has acquired the respect of other people. Her future is by no means clear, especially in terms of employment.

Area 5

CASE 1. Excellent attendance. He worked on Saturdays, Sundays and Wednesday evenings and finished his order in something like record time. His tasks were trowelling at an archaeological dig, helping the disabled to swim, providing an appraisal of the community service scheme to a blind student. Community service filled a vacuum in his life; his attendance and response were excellent and he is determined to continue his work on community service indefinitely.

His supervisors reported –

'I see the community service scheme offering him opportunities to call on talents which have hitherto been untapped. He appears to be an ideal person whenever involvement with children and handicapped persons is required. He has a notable understanding and sympathetic appreciation of their needs and quite obviously enjoys participating in activities with them. I hope and think that he is getting as much out of community service as community service is getting out of him and that the community service will continue without the order when the order is completed.'

'He has shown remarkable sympathy for, interest in and understanding of the patients involved and displays the marked degree of patience which is necessary to cope with the irregular situations that occur when working with the mentally sub-normal person. It is his intention, to my delight, to continue with the swimming sessions and I understand he will also be joining an organisation to continue community service. In my opinion community service has given him the opportunity to discover and realise the certain part of his make-up which has hitherto lain dormant.'

CASE 2. His attendance was excellent. He travelled by bus each Wednesday evening to his task – a lengthy journey, at a time when travelling difficulties had preoccupied the community service team. His tasks were assisting in swimming therapy, erecting fencing around play area, landscaping gardens, erecting stalls for fund-raising event, duties at an archaeological dig. His response was very positive indeed. He expressed a wish to perform community service at weekends and to continue his mid-week involvement at the swimming sessions after the completion of his order. Supervisors reported –

'Swimming with handicapped children – he really finds his feet in this activity. He obviously has a very sympathetic and understanding approach to the kids and is ideally suited to this type of project.'

'Fencing erection – tackled all aspects of the job eagerly and competently'.

'Stall erection at fete – freely offered his help at the fete and joined in whole-heartedly with all present'.

What distinguished the successes

Table 32
Offenders with satisfactorily completed orders, and with unsatisfactorily terminated orders as at June 30 1974

	Number of those with orders satisfactorily completed	Number of those with orders unsatisfactorily terminated*	Total number of those on whom orders made
Durham	32	12	99
Inner London	117	58	400
Kent	41	16	158
Nottingham	69	23	263
Shropshire	17	2	67
South-west Lancashire	31	3	185
All areas	307	114	1172

* Including those being breached.

Table 32 shows, by area, the number of orders satisfactorily completed and the number of orders unsatisfactorily terminated. The total number of those on whom orders were made up to June 30 1974 is included for purpose of comparison.

Dividing orders that have run for a year (i.e. those made January to June 1973) into orders that were completed or extended by the court, and those that terminated through breach or a further offence, it is possible to see whether the two groups of offenders differed in respect of their criminal record. Classifying them according to the nature of the offence for which they were put on community service, there was no significant relationship between the type of offence and manner of the order's termination ($X^2 = 2.73$, 3df).

If offenders are classified according to whether or not they had previously served a custodial sentence, it is found that those who had served such a sentence were significantly more likely to terminate their order unsatisfactorily than others ($X^2 = 13.09$, 1df, p $<.001$).

If the length of criminal record of those who had their order terminated in an unsatisfactory way is compared to the record of the others, those with unsatisfactory terminations are seen to have significantly longer criminal records ($X^2 = 7.37$, 1df, p $<.01$).

CHAPTER 5

Attitudes and Opinions about Community Service

Community service has created a great deal of interest amongst a variety of people. In any discussion of a new form of treatment, it is important to take into account the attitudes and opinions of those who are involved in or affected by the scheme. This chapter describes what sentencers, probation officers with responsibility for community service in the experimental areas, other probation officers, offenders, work-providing agencies, the press and others think about this new form of treatment.

Views of community service officers*

At the beginning of October 1973, one researcher interviewed the community service officer** of each of the six experimental areas. Their views are important as they have experience in the organisation of the scheme and are aware of the practical problems involved. They were asked questions of a fairly general nature to enable each officer to choose what he felt were the salient points for discussion. A copy of the questionnaire was sent to each of the officers several days before the tape-recorded interview took place.

All officers believed that responsibility for community service should remain with the probation and after-care service, and felt that their experience as probation officers had been useful in preparing them for their present job. However, it appeared that their training as probation officers had not sufficiently prepared them for all aspects of their work.

Some dissatisfactions for probation officers working in the community service scheme were mentioned, including the views that their special conditions and responsibilities need to be considered by the National Association of Probation Officers and that the specialist nature of the work leads to a feeling of isolation from other officers of the same grade. However, all the officers felt that being involved in a new scheme is satisfying for all members of staff.

The aims of community service which they mentioned were varied, but they all emphasised the benefit to be gained both by the offender and the community. The offender can gain a 'positive experience', as opposed to the negative one of imprisonment. He can learn to give rather than to take. None of the officers strongly believed that community service conflicted with the aims of the probation and after-care service. Two officers mentioned the difference in method from the traditional casework approach, feeling that this might cause some probation officers to be resistant towards the scheme.

---

* i.e. the officer in each experimental area with day-to-day responsibility for community service (known in London as the Director of the Community Service Centre).

** Except in Kent and London, the community service officers interviewed had been involved from the time the scheme was set up.

None of the officers saw the scheme's future as uncertain. They had all planned for it to extend beyond the experimental period. One officer felt that he would like to see the scheme expanded nationally but did not think that reliable results could be available for several years. To prevent the scheme from being isolated from the rest of the probation and after-care service, one officer thought that each group of probation officers should have a responsibility for it in their area, so that it could be seen as a normal part of their work load. Other possible changes to the scheme were outlined by the officer who suggested that, if community service offenders were also subject to outstanding fines, it could be advantageous to convert them to hours of community service because the availability of some clients for community service tasks is restricted by their need to work overtime to pay off fines. The view was expressed that the limits of hours ordered could be increased from the 40 to 240 fixed by the 1972 Act to 100 to 300 hours; one officer considered that 40 hours were too short, but he and four others thought 240 hours too long. If a third of the hours ordered was allowed for remission, as suggested by one officer, then loss of some of this, or weekend detention* might be a substitute for breach proceedings, which would then be taken only as a last resort.

When asked what was needed to ensure success of the scheme, they mentioned a variety of things including careful planning for the future; the maintenance of communication and liaison with interested bodies; and the beginning of grants to organisations providing work for the scheme.

Views of other probation officers

The views of other probation officers were examined because their attitude towards community service determines how many recommendations for this sentence are made in social inquiry reports. The community service officers had all encountered resistance towards the scheme amongst probation officers. Four of the six officers mentioned that misunderstanding of the scheme occurred among officers who failed to take advantage of the information offered them about the scheme. Some probation officers were simply uninterested, others disagreed with what they believe to be its aims. The view was expressed that some officers did not make recommendations for community service because of their uncertainty about it and, in particular, about the criteria for suitability.

In January 1974, a short questionnaire was sent to a sample of probation officers (selected randomly from staff lists) from five of the experimental areas. The aims of the survey were to discover:

---

* The following passage is in the Advisory Council on Penal System's recently published report: Young Adult Offenders [21]. ' . . . as community service develops consideration should be given to the possible value of residential centres from which community service projects could be operated and at which offenders could be ordered by the courts to spend their weekends' (paragraph 177).

1. what probation officers were prepared to recognise as advantages of the scheme,
2. how they saw the place of community service in relation to custodial and non-custodial sentences,
3. what disadvantages probation officers thought the scheme had and what reservations they had about it. (It was hoped that this might show the possible reasons for probation officers failing to make recommendations for community service).

Of the 239 officers in the sample, 179 (74·9%) returned their questionnaires.

One question comprised a list of general statements about community service.* Officers were asked to classify each statement as an advantage, a disadvantage, or neither, of the scheme. The statements were:

1. Community service leads the community to greater understanding of offenders.
2. Offenders on community service will come into contact with the recipients of their help.
3. Community service is preferable to a custodial sentence in many cases.
4. Society benefits from the community service work done by offenders.
5. Community service has therapeutic value.
6. Community service enables the offender to use his leisure time constructively.
7. Community service has punitive elements.
8. Community service gives offenders an opportunity to help others.
9. Community service gives offenders the opportunity to realise abilities previously untapped.
10. Offenders on community service work alongside non-offender volunteers.
11. Community service is a form of reparation to the community.

The only two items which more than three of the officers returning the questionnaire saw as disadvantages of the scheme were those numbered 7 (38 officers) and 11 (13 officers). Item 7 was the only one which less than half the officers were prepared to recognise as an advantage of the scheme. There was moderately high agreement between the areas in the ordering of statements, ranked according to the number of probation officers seeing each statement as an advantage of the scheme.**

Another question was designed to elicit the officers' views of the place of community service in relation to other methods of disposal. In examining the

---

* The statements were adapted from social enquiry reports which recommended the making of a community service order. They were not intended as a comprehensive list of supposed 'virtues' of the scheme.
**Kendall's Coefficient of Concordance $W = 0·48$ p $<$ ·01.

Table 33

Probation Officers' views of Community Service in relation to other disposals.

Probation Officer regards Community Service as	Probation Officer regards a suspended sentence as custodial				Probation Officer regards a suspended sentence as non-custodial			
	Primarily an alternative to a custodial sentence	Primarily an alternative to a non-custodial sentence	An alternative to either custodial or non-custodial sentence	A sentence in its own right	Primarily an alternative to a custodial sentence	Primarily an alternative to a non-custodial sentence	An alternative to either custodial or non-custodial sentence	A sentence in its own right
Durham	4	0	2	8	3	0	6	9
Kent	10	0	1	3	6	0	8	10
Nottingham	15	0	2	7	11	1	3	9
Shropshire	2	0	2	3	0	0	6	3
South-west Lancashire	5	0	4	10	2	0	7	5
All areas	36	0	11	31	22	1	30	36

answers, the sample was split according to whether officers regarded a suspended sentence as custodial (78 officers) or non-custodial (89 officers).* Table 33 shows the results broken down in this way. Assuming that those who describe community service as 'a sentence in its own right' will not restrict their recommendation of it to offenders who are likely to receive a custodial sentence, 54% of officers who regarded a suspended sentence as custodial, and 74% of officers who regarded a suspended sentence as non-custodial, considered community service as an alternative to non-custodial as well as to custodial sentences. The two groups were further sub-divided according to whether or not the probation and after-care areas concerned considered community service only as an alternative to custody. It was found that by and large officers' views of community service in the range of sentencing alternatives did not correspond very closely to their area's expressed view.

The final question invited officers to criticise the scheme, and some interesting replies were received. The points made can be placed into six broad categories which are given below together with a selection of quotations.**

Dissatisfaction with the scheme at present
Most of the criticisms came into this category, some being directed to the philosophy behind the scheme e.g.:

'It is based on the old assumption that if one exposes the CRIMINAL to good people, influences etc., his malformed character will be modified by the experience. It is essentially a moralistic assumption, concentrating on the individual regardless of his situation, and continues to prolong the divisive nature of our society.'

However, most of the criticism in this category concerned aspects of the scheme in the officer's area, e.g.:

Concerning the type of work available:
'There is not enough variety in the choice of things to do ...' and, 'community service doesn't always provide the type of work that was envisaged by the person recommending it';

Concerning communication:
'Lack of precise knowledge as to what is to be the actual work done (and where) when recommending a community service order in a social inquiry report ... Resulting complete lack of contact when order is made/served ...';

Concerning type of offender considered suitable for community service:
'... the scheme appears to be directed towards working class clients and is not seen as suitable for middle class offenders.'

---

* Excluding 12 probation officers who did not state how they regarded a suspended sentence.

** The quotations have been selected to represent the range of criticisms encountered and to exclude quotations in which individual areas can be identified.

Attitude of courts towards community service

Many comments made came into this category, e.g.:

'There seems to be ambiguity in interpretation amongst magistrates and judges in the higher courts'; and,

'Lack of uniformity in awarding community service orders in the courts . . .'; or,

'My main reservation about community service lies . . . with . . . the seemingly minimal impact it has made on our sentencers . . . I am a little disturbed at the way magistrates have utilised community service in instances where a custodial sentence was not contemplated in the first instance.'

It was felt that where criticisms were levelled at the use made of community service by the courts, or the way the scheme is organised in the officer's area, this may show why at least some officers are unwilling or reluctant to make more recommendations for community service. The other comments made could be placed in the following categories:

Reservations about the way the scheme could develop

For example:

'If the number of hours for community service allowed to be imposed is too great, it could become too punitive'; and,

'It may become too task-orientated, and once the choice of task is made there may be insufficient "casework" done with the offender'.

The place of community service in the range of sentencing alternatives

Four types of comment came into this category:

Those from officers who felt that community service should be an alternative to custody only:

'Community service orders should, in my mind, be limited, for the time being at least, . . . to those persons who really are at risk of going to prison . . .';

Those who felt that it should be aimed at a wider population:

'I feel that the scheme should be fully available to *all* offenders, and not just those about to go to an institution . . .';

Those who felt that community service should be linked to supervision of some kind:

'. . . community service offenders should be divided into those receiving supervision and those who do not, i.e. there should be an alternative form of community service supervision order';

and some who felt that it should remain separate from supervision:

'. . . the tendency to move towards "supervision with a community service order" . . . would be detrimental . . . a community service order should stand alone'.

The extension of the scheme

The few officers who discussed this were mainly those who were anxious lest it should go national too soon e.g.:

'There is a danger that community service will be extended nationally as a political expedient without a full appraisal of the pilot schemes . . .'.

How the scheme could be improved and how to ensure its success

One of the ideas put forward was that community service should be

'extended to age groups 15 to 17 years where intermediate treatment does not have the punitive elements the client sometimes requires'.

Another survey of the attitudes of probation officers towards community service was conducted by two students of the University of Bath, who interviewed 26 officers from Shropshire[22]. They found that 18 of the officers in their sample felt that the legislation was well timed: only one officer felt that it was premature, and seven said that it was overdue. When the officers were given a list of possible aims of the scheme (to choose as many as they wished), 15 said treatment, 15 retribution, 11 punishment, 9 prison relief, 5 rehabilitation, 4 integration of the offender with the community, 3 cost, and 1 tolerance of the offender by the community. When asked if they would be prepared to recommend community service in lieu of various other sentences, 23 would recommend it instead of detention centre, 16 instead of borstal, 25 instead of prison, 17 instead of fines, and 4 instead of probation. The only offences which a considerable number (14) regarded as precluding this sentence were sex offences.

Views of sentencers

No direct information about sentencers' attitudes towards community service is available at present, but local research is being carried out in Durham which should provide useful data. However, replies received to the survey of probation officers' attitudes towards community service in the experimental areas suggest that some officers may be reluctant to recommend this sentence because of the attitude of the court towards the scheme.

One officer wished that courts would ask for specific reports on those they intended to place on community service, instead of making deductions from social reports that had been prepared without consideration of this particular form of disposal. Other officers felt that the possibilities of the scheme were not yet well enough appreciated by some courts, despite such arrangements as had been made to inform them about the new form of treatment.

A form was devised to be completed by a probation officer in all cases where a community service order was considered, at any stage in the sentencing process, whether or not an order was made. On the form was a space for a précis of remarks made by the sentencer when passing sentence. These remarks do not appear to show any commonly held reservations about the scheme. Most of the remarks told the offender the conditions of the order. He was often told, sometimes forcefully, that he was lucky to have escaped a custodial sentence.

Views of offenders

A small sample of offenders from the intake of the Inner London, Kent and South-west Lancashire schemes was interviewed over a five week period during June and July 1973. Each offender was to be interviewed twice, at his initial meeting with the community service officer, and again after he had completed at least 30 hours of his order. It was hoped that the latter interview would show if the offender then realised more fully the implications of a community service order, in comparison to his initial impression of the scheme. Unfortunately, fewer than half the sample could be interviewed a second time. (Of the 18 offenders interviewed in Inner London, six were seen a second time; neither of the two offenders interviewed in Kent was re-interviewed; and only four of the seven offenders interviewed in South-west Lancashire were interviewed again).

Positive points from the interviews were:

1. Although the scheme is designed to deprive offenders of part of their leisure time, it is apparent that the majority interviewed have no constructive leisure pursuits. In fact, most of them said that they would have been doing 'nothing special' had they not been doing this work.

2. At the initial interview, most offenders understood something of the motives behind a community service order but would have benefited from more details, especially in writing.

3. They seemed grateful for the chance to avoid a custodial sentence (where this was envisaged), and determined to make a success of the sentence.

4. The majority thought the sentence fair.

5. Community service seems to provide both a routine and an interest for offenders who are unemployed.

6. Some found it difficult to understand how the work they were doing was of value to the community.

7. Those working for voluntary agencies seemed to get on well with their supervisors and appreciated their interest.

8. The majority of those seen for a second time felt that the experience of community service had been worthwhile and had helped them in some way even if only to 'keep me off the streets'.

9. They obviously saw community service as a more positive sentence than imprisonment*.

A probation officer in Nottingham conducted semi-structured interviews to determine the views of some offenders immediately after they had finished their order. She interviewed successfully 20 of them, but 14 other interviews were

---

* Further details of the survey from which these points were extracted are available from the Home Office Research Unit on request.

unproductive and 6 were awaited. There have been some interesting findings from the 20 successful interviews, 14 felt that they had served the community and only one did not think he had. All but two claimed that, knowing what they then knew, they would still have agreed to community service. If this sentence had not existed, 13 felt that they would have received a custodial sentence, two a fine and two probation or another sentence. 15 saw community service as an alternative to imprisonment; 17 felt that probation would have been of less benefit to them; and 17 felt that their community service experience had been worthwhile. Only two of the 20 had been involved in community work before their sentence, but 12 were after their experience of community service and these intended to continue with the work. An important aspect to emerge has been the development of the relationship between the offender and his supervisor, although no direct questions were asked about this. Of the 11 offenders who mentioned supervisors, nine spoke in very positive terms, and two in negative terms. The East Midlands Branch of the National Association of Probation Officers has commented that these positive attitudes of offenders 'must be a reason for viewing this scheme with some optimism' (personal communication).

There has been a great deal of informal contact between the Research Unit and offenders on community service. In each of the experimental areas, at least one researcher has worked with offenders on community service tasks. Researchers have also participated in the day-to-day activities of five of the community service offices, including attendance at offenders' interviews.

One offender, when asked at his initial interview with the community service officer what he thought of the scheme replied, 'Anything's better than prison'. He did not want hard manual work but he liked people and wanted to help handicapped children, organise games, swimming, etc. In the same area, after working with two offenders on a project, the supervisor commented 'Generally speaking, both worked well, although they expressed dislike of working on Sundays and "not getting paid for it".' In another area, one offender said that '. . . he enjoyed community service work and as he was unemployed it made a pleasant change from sitting at home.'

One final comment to close this section came from an offender who had just spent a hard day helping to move soil ready for a pathway. The community service officer who had been working with him asked if he had a great feeling of satisfaction at all the good work he had done. The offender leaned on his shovel and said, 'No, I just feel tired.'

Views of work-providing agencies

All the community service officers said that, in general, finding work was not a problem: the problem was rather the fact that too few orders were being made to take advantage of all the job opportunities. However, finding the right *type* of work could be a problem, e.g. work available on Sundays, or in the client's local community. Also, work placements involving personal relationships with beneficiaries of service have not always been available. In at least two areas there were initial difficulties in getting the local authority to provide work, but eventually tasks were made available.

One of the experimental areas gave the researchers a complete dossier of contacts made with possible work-providing agencies (excluding several who had not replied to the initial letter). The contacts began in October 1972 and usually involved a meeting with a representative of the agency concerned, at which community service was explained in some detail. From such meetings it was determined whether the agency would be able to provide suitable work for offenders, and also what was the attitude of the agency towards community service and to the use of offenders generally. In many cases, more than one meeting was needed before a decision was reached, because the proposal had to be put to a committee or because more information was required. Some agency representatives wanted time to think about the implications of the scheme, or practical issues such as insurance had to be clarified. Some agencies simply did not have suitable work for offenders. During the period October 1972 to January 1974, 152 agencies were approached. Of these, 54 reacted favourably and were able to provide work, and a further 76 were favourable but the provision of work was uncertain. Of the remainder, five were unfavourable but open to further negotiations, one was unfavourable and not open to any further negotiation, and with 16 there was no clear outcome. Thus the reception of the idea of community service ranged in nearly all cases from great enthusiasm to willingness to give the scheme a trial.

Discussion sometimes modified initial opposition to the idea of the scheme; for example, with one representative whose first reaction was 'I don't think our members will want to work with people like that.' The member of another organisation, who had the most reservations about community service during a meeting, was the one who after it suggested further possible contacts for the scheme.

The interviews with the community service officers gave some indication of the attitudes of voluntary agencies towards community service. The main reason for agencies being reluctant to participate appeared to be their feelings towards offenders working as volunteers; for example, one organisation had had unhappy experience in using borstal boys. Alternatively, they may feel threatened by the thought of using offenders, or that the good name of the agency would be contaminated by doing so. On the other hand, the agency may simply have wanted to wait until it had seen the scheme in operation before committing itself. There may be many reasons why an agency might be reluctant to continue in the scheme, but the main one is probably a bad experience with clients on community service orders. For this reason, two officers mentioned that careful assessment or matching is necessary before clients are placed with agencies.*

---

* One agency which withdrew from the scheme was asked in confidence for its reasons for withdrawal, but was not willing to give them.

Despite difficulties encountered with some agencies, enough are pre, co-operate with the scheme to ensure provision of enough work.

Views of trade unions

Before the scheme began, attention was given to the likely views of the trade unions. The Trades Union Congress was consulted by the Home Office and endorsed the arrangements; and each of the six experimental areas was given the name of a local trade union representative to contact. These contacts have been of varying usefulness. Another way of developing contacts between community service organisers and trade unions has been the appointment of trade union representatives to the community service sub-committee of the probation and after-care committees in some areas.

In the event, difficulties in this area have been few, and where they occurred, were usually raised by representatives at individual work places. These have been resolved at local level by probation representatives. A general principle of community service work has been that it is work that would not otherwise have been done at all. Obviously this rule is not proof against abuse, but it is likely to help trade union acceptance.

Views expressed in the press

Examination of press reports on community service gives an indication of how the public's attitudes towards the scheme are formed. From January 1973 use was made of a press cutting agency, which extracted information relating to community service from an extensive list of 'newspapers, periodicals and con-sumer magazines published in the United Kingdom'. There are some local newspapers from which the agency does not extract, and radio and television are not covered. The coverage achieved is comprehensive of national newspapers and very wide among local newspapers, and allows useful general deductions to be made.

Content analysis of the press cuttings so obtained between January and Sept-ember 1973 revealed that editorial comment in national and local newspapers was very largely favourable towards the scheme. Reservations expressed in editorials concerned the administration rather than the principle of the scheme, especially the nature of the work performed on community service and the category of offender for which it is appropriate.

Throughout the period under study, community service has been described as an alternative to various other types of disposal. Before the scheme started, 11 of the 12 press items seen mentioned community service as an alternative ex-clusively to custody. During the first nine months of 1973, the bulk of press reports of community service (27 out of 42) mentioned the sentence as an alternative only to custody. After September 1973 almost all press cuttings re-ceived described individual court cases. This may also account for the relatively small number of reports which mention breach procedure, only one before the scheme started and 13 afterwards.

The following five aims of community service were distinguished in the cuttings received:

1. Cheaper alternative to imprisonment and a way to relieve overcrowding in prisons.
2. Leads to personal change and rehabilitation of offenders.
3. Allows the offender to continue in his employment.
4. Punishment elements are intrinsic in the scheme (excluding mention of possible breach proceedings).
5. The work done benefits the community.

The description of those suitable for community service and the offences mentioned of those sentenced to community service are consistent with the circumstances envisaged in the Wootton Report.

Published views in opposition to the scheme

Although much has been written in favour of community service, only three articles are known to the writers that opposed the scheme and they do not contain criticisms of operation. A magistrate writing about the cost of the project is one[23]:

'It has now leaked out that this penalty . . . will cost £100,000 (and who believes official estimates? We've been caught so many times before!) and all to what purpose? All to try and make silk purses out of sows' ears!'

A representative of Radical Alternatives to Imprisonment when writing about the scheme in one area said:

'Given the political causes of crime and inequality of distribution of resources and opportunity, it is doubtful that those who have rejected the normative system of the middle class will see the error of their ways and remould their actions accordingly as a result of the operations of another manifestation of the same system . . . Any allocated task is likely to reflect middle class objectives and values, possibly illustrated by the present preoccupation with environmental problems. Such tasks are unlikely to commend themselves to the working class offender who is likely to see more immediate personal and social problems as having priority'.[24]*

A former prison governor stated that[25]:

'If this type of voluntary work is to be effective it will obviously need the co-operation of the criminal (or offender – call him what you will). So one

---

* The representative has since admitted that the comments quoted above were 'from limited experience' and 'merely preliminary thoughts'.

must presume him to have attributes of nobility, integrity and selflessness – albeit well hidden beneath his more apparent characteristics of greed, avarice, remorselessness and abject self-interest'.

He was also pessimistic about the likelihood of the young offender attending regularly for work:

'. . . following the example of his elders, who play truant from work (euphemistically called striking – either official or unofficial) he follows suit and plays truant from school. Also encouraged by his elders who never perform anything, other than the reflex actions of living, without estimating the material reward, the young scallywag is not likely to give up his own time for nothing'.

The quotations are included because of their diversity. No community service scheme could conceivably meet the objections committed to print.

Views of the National Association of Probation Officers and the British Association of Social Workers

Any account of expressed attitudes towards community service would be incomplete without a reference to the views of the National Association of Probation Officers (N.A.P.O.) and the British Association of Social Workers (B.A.S.W.), as their members are concerned with the operation of the scheme. In response to a request from the Research Unit for comments on the subject of community service, a representative of the East Midlands branch of N.A.P.O. wrote:

'We would not be surprised if your report drew attention to a differentiation between the experimental areas in the type of project they placed their offenders with. The Nottingham City and County area is able we understand to call upon a large number of voluntary bodies. Others area may not have been so fortunate in the degree to which they were accorded this co-operation. However, it would obviously appear desirable when offenders are able to work for their community through agencies which that particular community is responsible for.

Another area of concern has been the question of whether offenders are in fact made subject to a community service order when their only alternative was a period of imprisonment. We trust that your research may throw some light on this important issue. The problem for probation officers is that community service orders are of benefit if they reduce the prison population. It would therefore be of value if this principle was reasserted. However, many probation officers are also aware that community service orders can assist offenders who do not fall into this category, although these schemes may only work if they are entirely voluntary from the offender's point of view.

. . . N.A.P.O. wishes to be positive in its attitude to this scheme and will therefore await your research findings with interest, as matters for improvement will no doubt be highlighted. We are of the opinion that it would be of harm to the whole concept of community service orders in the future if problems that have emerged are not rectified at this stage'.

The Assistant General Secretary of B.A.S.W. has written that it believes it is crucial that community service orders are maintained as an alternative to a custodial sentence, although there is:

'a case for developing community service for other offenders, but this should be done on a voluntary basis as a supplement to the penalty imposed by courts e.g. probation, fine etc.'.

'There is scope for local variation in the development of community service ... (but) ... it is important that the service undertaken is seen by the client as making a direct contribution to the needs of the community. In this way, the reparative element of community service can be emphasised'.

It feels that weaknesses in the legislation have emerged and any extension of the scheme could benefit by taking these into account:

'The maximum sentence of 240 hours ... can pose real difficulties for a man in full time employment ... we would suggest that two or three terms, possibly 100, 150 or 200 hours, should be set. The court would then be able to make its choice according to the needs and abilities of the offender in the same way as it selects the term of a probation order'.

It believes that community service orders should be dischargeable for good progress (as is already so for most of the supervision undertaken by the probation and after-care service). It hopes that:

'opportunities for service involving interpersonal relationships would be available when appropriate. The possibility of community service leading on to involvement in projects like New Careers is one of the most welcome elements in the scheme'.

In conclusion, the B.A.S.W. stated:

'We would therefore support an extension of the scheme to all probation areas if the research findings support our impression that community service has made a contribution in reducing the numbers of offenders in custody, and in offering a constructive alternative to sentences'.

CHAPTER 6

Possible Changes in the Scheme

The legal framework

The community service scheme is new, and it is natural that some difficulties should occur in interpreting the statutory provisions (ss. 14 to 17 of the Powers of Criminal Courts Act 1973), and in adapting practice to a novel situation. As the preceding chapters show, the scheme has made a good start in the six experimental areas.

The researchers did not attempt to examine in detail the working of the legal provisions or discuss them with clerks to justices or sentencers: the probation officers concerned did, however, mention a few grounds for concern lest the statutory background of community service should work less than smoothly. For example they said that arrangements for revocation of community service orders, and for action on an order when the subject of it was convicted by a different court for a further offence, were not so convenient as those applicable to probation orders.* As mentioned in Chapter 5, five of the six community service officers believed that the 240 maximum permissible hours were excessive. Some officers said there were doubts about the way in which the range of permissible hours, 40 to 240, under section 14(1) of the 1973 Act, should be interpreted when orders in respect of two or more offences were in operation simultaneously, and under which of such orders breach proceedings could properly be instituted. There was some uncertainty, natural in a form of treatment that is necessarily so vaguely specified, about what would constitute satisfactory evidence of breach. And one or two suggestions, that have from time to time been made in other connections, were repeated, in particular that a court should have a written social inquiry report (before making a community service order), and that magistrates should be eligible for co-option (to community service committees).

Finally, a point was made in connection with an officer's obligation, under section 15(3) of the 1973 Act, to avoid giving instructions to an offender that conflict with his normal hours of work. It was suggested that a community service order should impose an obligation to acquaint the relevant officer with alterations in working hours due to change in employment (or overtime), as the less work-orientated probation order normally does.

Other views of those who operate the scheme

1. Some of those on community service have to work overtime to pay off outstanding fines, and this affects their availability for community service work. To overcome this, when a man is sentenced to community service any outstanding fines could be translated into hours of community service. Similarly, community service organisers tend to see as self-defeating the simultaneous imposition by a court of a fine and a community service order.

---

* This is especially so in the case of orders made in a Crown Court.

2. There is considerable support for the decentralisation of the community service scheme, the extreme suggestion being that one probation officer in each probation office in an area be responsible for the development of community service in that locality. (Incidentally, some probation officers in the experimental areas have involved probationers voluntarily in community service tasks).

3. Given the mutual dependence of work-providing agencies and the probation and after-care service in the development of community service, there is support for the view that the service should make development grants, as necessary, to voluntary organisations[26]. Probation and after-care committees can, under the Powers of Criminal Courts Act 1973 (Sch. 3, para. 10(3)(c)), 'make payments to any society or body in respect of services rendered by them' in relation to community service orders; but such payments cannot take the form of grants to stimulate or sustain the general activities of the society or body. There is some anxiety that community service may come to be seen as a cheap alternative to prison and thus not be funded in a way which would allow it to develop to its limits.

CHAPTER 7

Summary and Conclusions

Chapter 1: Background to the Community Service Scheme

1. The background to the community service scheme in the Wootton Report, a Home Office working group, and the Criminal Justice Act, 1972 is briefly described. The aims, methods and limitations of the research in six experimental probation and after-care areas are set out.

2. The rationale of community service is examined. Its appeal to adherents of different penal philosophies, and the argument about whether this fact provides the scheme with its greatest potential or is a symptom of confusion in the aims of the scheme are discussed. The scheme's casting of the offender in the role of helper rather than helped is mentioned.

Chapter 2: Suitability of Offenders for Community Service

3. The place of community service in the range of sentences is briefly discussed. In three of the six probation and after-care areas community service is regarded as more or less exclusively an alternative to a custodial sentence.

4. Statements from probation and after-care areas about criteria of suitability for community service are presented. Many of them exclude certain categories of offender, e.g. the sexual offender, rather than specify suitability in positive terms.

5. A content analysis of social inquiry reports recommending community service and those not recommending community service is briefly described. The results of the analysis were inconclusive.

6. A sentencing exercise conducted with probation officers in three of the experimental areas is described. It showed that:

   (a) Of the 55 officers interviewed, 38 (69%) recommend that the offender chosen as the community service case should be given community service. The recommendation for community service was less frequent when open consideration was asked for rather than consideration specifically for community service.

   (b) There was general agreement between probation officers as to what was important for them to know about offenders when reaching a view about a suitable sentence. Judged importance of different categories of information was similar whether the sentence under consideration was community service or some other sentence.

   (c) There was a variety of reasons for recommending community service.

   (d) In all three of the areas studied the officers regarded information about an offender's medical history as more important when considering community service than when choosing between different treatments.

Officers in one area regarded drug usage, interests and activities, and personality as each more important in community service consideration than in consideration of other sentences.

(e) Factors, within each of the general topics, favourable and unfavourable to a community service recommendation are listed.

Chapter 3: The Practice of Community Service

7. Typically a community service order followed a probation officer's recommendation of that sentence. The courts' take-up rates of recommendations for community service varied between areas, but the average was probably not lower than that in relation to probation.

8. Not all community service orders were made in cases where a custodial sentence would otherwise have been passed, but it is not possible at present to estimate with certainty the number that were.

9. There were area differences in the philosophy and administration of the scheme.

10. The number of orders made differed between areas, but when corrected for the size of the probation and after-care area, it seems that the smaller schemes were not under-developed relative to the larger areas.

11. There were differences between individual courts in the proportion of long (150 hours plus) orders made. The Crown Court in three areas made disproportionately more long orders than magistrates' courts. In a fourth area the converse was true.

12. Offenders on community service were drawn primarily from the 17 to 24 age range.

3. Rates at which orders were made were sensitive to local difficulties and lack of publicity. Fluctuations in these rates are attributable more to fluctuations in umber of probation officer recommendations of community service than to uctuations in number of initiations of community service consideration by courts.

14. Community service work was usually done in the company of volunteers or beneficiaries of service or both.

15. A wide diversity of tasks was undertaken on community service.

16. Except in one area, more community service work was done at weekends than on weekdays.

17. The average time taken to complete an order of 240 hours was near enough to the year allowed to give cause for concern about longer orders.

18. The average (median) number of previous convictions of those ordered to undertake community service was three in some areas, four in the others.

19. Between 38% and 50% of offenders on community service had had experience of a custodial sentence.

20. Typically the offender on community service had committed a property offence. His most frequent previous offence was also a property offence; but there were a number doing community service who had typically committed offences against the person, motoring offences or other offences.

Chapter 4: Success and Failure on Community Service

21. Difficulties of principle in defining unsuccessful termination of orders are discussed, calling attention to differences between areas in defining when it was appropriate to ask the court to vary or terminate an order.

22. Successes of the scheme are presented.

23. Numbers of successful and unsuccessful terminations of orders are presented for each area.

24. It is shown that those with longer criminal records, and those who had served a custodial sentence, were less likely to terminate their order by completing it. Type of offence committed was not found to predict manner of an order's discharge.

Chapter 5: Attitudes and Opinions towards Community Service

25. Development of community service needs the acceptance of the scheme by all concerned. The scheme's fullest success depends upon the readiness of probation officers to recommend offenders for community service and of courts to make orders; upon offenders' co-operation with the terms of the order; and upon public acceptance of the measure and agencies' willingness to provide the right kinds of work in sufficient quantity.

26. In at least one of the experimental areas, a majority of probation officers regard the introduction of community service in 1972 as well-timed or overdue. The majority of probation officers in five of the experimental areas recognised a number of advantages in the scheme, and some have criticised the scheme at a number of levels. Most of the officers in the sample regarded community service as an alternative to non-custodial as well as custodial sentences, but there was variation between the areas.

27. Sentencers' remarks when passing sentence do not indicate any commonly held reservations about the scheme, but it is possible that some probation officers have been reluctant to make a recommendation for community service because of the way they thought sentencers saw the scheme.

Many offenders on community service had positive attitudes towards the scheme, and there was for the time being sufficient work to employ them.

29. The scheme has met with little published opposition, and has usually been

described in the press as an alternative to custody. The scheme has generally had a good press, often being presented as a means of reducing the prison population.

30. There has been no general, and little local, difficulty in relationships with trade unions.

Chapter 6: Possible Changes in the Scheme

31. Difficulties arising from the legal framework of the scheme or its interpretation are mentioned. Notable amongst these are the current arrangements for revocation of an order. The procedure is particularly clumsy in the case of orders made in the Crown Court.

32. The views of those who operate the scheme, on its direction of development, are given. There is considerable support for the decentralisation of the administration of the community service scheme.

In conclusion

The community service experience shows that the scheme is viable; orders are being made and completed, sometimes evidently to the benefit of the offenders concerned. However, the effect on the offenders as a whole is as yet unknown; the penal theory underlining the scheme is thought by some to be uncertain; it has not as yet made much impact on the prison population because of the manner of its use by the courts; in practice a few supervisors may be able to subvert some orders of the court unless good contact at the work-site is maintained by the probation and after-care service; and neither the type of offender for whom it is suitable, nor the most desirable work placements for different individuals on community service are as yet known. The writers feel much more optimistic about the scheme than this list implies, but have tried throughout not to state the case for community service any more strongly than the evidence currently available justifies. Even so, the scheme is at least viable; and it is intended to get a clearer picture of its outcome (in the short-term) in mid-1975, by examining the one-year reconviction rates of offenders made subject to orders during the first year of the operation of the scheme in each of the experimental areas. At best, community service is an exciting departure from traditional penal treatment.

BIBLIOGRAPHY

1. Criminal Justice Act 1972, and Powers of Criminal Courts Act 1973. London HMSO.

2. Non-custodial and Semi-custodial Penalties. Report of the Advisory Council on the Penal System. London, HMSO 1970.

3. Parliamentary Debates, Vol. 826, 22 November 1971, col. 972.

4. Parliamentary Debates, Standing Committee G, Criminal Justice Bill 12th Sitting, 8 February 1972, cols. 481–2.

5. Bailey W.C. Correctional Outcome. An evaluation of 100 Reports. *Journal of Criminal Law, Criminology and Police Science*. 1966, S7, (155–160).

6. Hauser R. Prison Reform and Society. *Prison Service Journal*. 1963, 3/9, (2–18).

7. Cohen S. Folk Devils and Moral Panics. London, MacGibbon and Kee 1972.

8. Del Vecchio G. The Struggle against Crime, in Acton H.B. (ed.). The Philisophy of Punishment. London, Macmillan 1969.

9. Gibbens T. Treatment at Liberty. *Annals of International Criminology* 1970, 9/1, (9–30).

10. Community Service Orders. A progress report of the first twelve months of Community Service by Offenders in County Durham. Durham County Probation and After-Care Service 1974. [Price on application. Final evaluation also available.]

11. Knapman E. Community Service Orders: A rationale. *Justice of the Peace* 23.3.74.

12. Thomas D.A. Principles of Sentencing. London, Heinemann 1970.

13. *Criminal Justice Act 1972. Community Service by Offenders. Information Bulletin No. 5. Inner London Probation and After-Care Service. December 1972.

14. *Criminal Justice Act 1972. Sections which apply to the operation of Community Service Orders. Nottingham Probation and After-Care Service. June 1974.

15. *Community Service by Offenders: Pilot Scheme. Durham Probation and After-Care Service. December 1972.

16. *Community Service Orders: Interim Report. Kent Probation and After-Care Service. February 1973.

17. *Community Service Orders: Pilot Scheme. Interim Report. South-West Lancashire Probation and After-Care Service. May 1974.

18. Wilkins L.T. and Chandler A. Confidence and Competence in the Decision-making process. British Journal of Criminology vol. 15(1) 1965.

19. Carter R.M. The Presentence Report and the Decision-making Process. *Journal of Research in Crime and Delinquency*. vol. 4(4) 1967.

20. Carter R.M. It is respectfully Recommended . . . *Federal Probation* (June) 1966.

21. Report of the Advisory Council on the Penal System. Young Adult Offenders. HMSO 1974.

22. Rose J. and McDuell R. The views of Shropshire probation officers concerning community service orders. Unpublished manuscript. University of Bath Department of Sociology 1974.

23. Anthony E. Legalised Waste. *Justice of the Peace.* 21 July 1973.

24. Uglow S. Community Service in Inner London – An Exercise in Illusion. Radical Alternatives to Prison. June 1973.

25. Bride G.F. Community Service Orders. *Justice of the Peace.* 2 June 1973.

26. *Simpson A. Keeping Pace with Topsy. Unpublished paper, Nottingham Council of Social Service. May 1973.

 *Not available

APPENDIX I

Information used in sentencing exercise

Topic	Community Service Case	Probation Case
Marital Situation	Engaged Wedding arranged for two months time	Single
Reaction to Previous Sentences	Seems to have settled down after last offence and has stopped going out with his brothers	No information
Medical History	No problems	Speech impediment – otherwise no trouble
Appearance	Average	Nothing abnormal
Siblings	Six brothers – one at home (mentally handicapped). Two sisters – away from home	Sister – 16 yrs. – lives at home. Brother – 24 yrs. – married and lives away
Education	Secondary school Left at 15 years	Attended secondary school where he achieved very little. Left at the age of 15 years
Age	21 years	19 years
Family Relationships	Good	Poor

Topic	Community Service Case	Probation Case
Personality	Friendly and co-operative Pleasant with open manner Honest during enquiries	Pleasant and apparently frank, but shows evidence of a weak personality
Peers	No information	Seeks approval from friends
Interests and Activities	Spends most of his time with fiancee	Virtually no leisure-time activities apart from drinking with friends
Employment History	Two years as a slaughterman three years in various labouring jobs. Made redundant after 18 months in last labouring job. Unemployed for four months until present job	Six months painting and decorating Two years window cleaning Six months steel fixing Two months window cleaning
Offence	Enter building as a trespasser with intent to steal. Offence occurred shortly after his father's death. His mother had a funeral bill for £84. All the brothers had to contribute and he was out of work at the time. It was to get this money that he broke into a Club	Taking motor vehicle without owner's consent Driving whilst disqualified No insurance Obstructing a police officer
Previous Convictions	Three previous court appearances as an adult – each time involved with older brothers. Convictions for assault in 1969 and threatening behaviour in 1972 relate to arguments in public houses that he and his brothers were involved in. Suspended sentence still in operation. No former custodial sentences	*Juvenile* – Four Two for theft One for damage to cement mixer One for using catapult *Adult* – Eight Six against Road Traffic Act One for obstructing Police One for using indecent language ALL THE ABOVE DEALT WITH BY *FINES*
Family Criminality	Older brothers Four have appeared in court on several occasions. One brother at present in prison	None

Topic	Community Service Case	Probation Case
Father	Coal miner until 1958 when ill-health forced him to give up work He suffered from bronchitis and asthma and was bed-ridden for several years. He died two months ago	Aged 55 years Long service in the army Now a manual worker in industry Strict
Drugs	No record of drug usage	No record of drug usage
Home	Council house Reasonable conditions	Three bedroom council house on a large housing estate Furnishing adequate Cleanliness – OK
Reaction to Present Offence	Fully realises seriousness of offence and is expecting prison sentence. In view of this he has postponed his wedding plans	Very worried as to the possible outcome
Drink	Has stopped drinking since he became engaged	Drinks beer regularly Eased off somewhat because of financial situation
Intelligence	Below average intelligence	Low intelligence IQ = 85. Much of his irresponsible behaviour seems to stem from his low intellect
Finance	Wage = £26 p.w. Pays £5 board	£1 – board £1 50p ⎬ fines – 50p ⎭ £69 outstanding Income = £4.39
Mother	62 years Forceful and dominant personality	Early 50s Works full time – Woolworths Does not know how to deal with son
Present Employment	Started work last month as a labourer	Unemployed for 10 months

APPENDIX II

Community service tasks performed

Inner London

Driving bus to Blackheath, Driving lorry for community care project, Driving, Constructing children's playground, Roof laying, Painting and decorating, Plastering, Electrical work, Glazing, Fixing fire doors, Clerical work, Leaflet distribution, Kitchen helper, Serving old age pensioners' lunches, Oxyacetylene cutting, Blazing, Burning rubbish, Bagging and distributing coal, Cooking, Canteen supervision, Cementing, Carpentry, Carpet laying, Window cleaning, Assisting in junior club, House repairs, Play leadership at play centre, Wall demolition, Assisting handicapped swimmers, Ambulance escort, Helping with fiesta, Carnival steward, Making coffee and washing up, Preparing and manning playgroup, Supervising boys club, Play leadership at play centre, Supervising youth club equipment and apparatus, Organising games at youth club, Escorting and assisting handicapped, Helping in youth club, Bricklaying and cementing, Repairing church fence, Gardening, Collecting and sorting waste paper, Demolition, Site clearance, Playing with children, Organising firework display, Stacking timber, Constructing an aviary, Fireproofing, Helping with jumble sale, Catering for Christmas, Laying paving stones, Lino laying, Roofing, Toy repairs, Mending fences, Clearing leaves, Assisting in Mother & Baby Club, Hospital visiting, Organising children's games, Organising children's camps, General office duties, Woodwork with disturbed children, Supervising junior soccer team, Repairing holiday hut for deprived children, Volunteer at night shelter, Cleaning, Sorting stores, Demolition of greenhouse.

Nottingham

Working in hospital, Decorating, Bricklaying, Building renovation, Concreting, Painting, Cleaning, Building maintenance, Household duties, Gardening, Land restoration, Canal clearance, Help at camp, Helping in youth club, Driving, Cleaning invalid cars, Visiting old people, Cleaning flats, Moving furniture, Furniture delivery, Removal work, Woodwork, Sawing wood, Clearing scrap metal, Site clearance, Bingo caller, Repairing toys, Making toys, Labouring, Floorlaying, Canteen help, Coffee bar attendant, Cooking, Cooking for OAPs, Weightlifting coaching, Shaving patients, Helping handicapped, Helping handicapped at home, Plastering, Moving coal for OAPs, re-wiring, Cutting nettles, Kitchen work, Ambulance cleaning, Metal work, Erecting fence, Archaeological excavation, Table tennis supervision, Replacing roof tiles, Visiting old people, Helping at children's picnic. Driving, Helping disabled in sports club, Driving coach for disabled, Swimming instruction, Boxing instruction, Bathing old people, Shopping for old people, Assisting youth leader, Assisting at playgroup, Help with jumble sale, Looking after a handicapped child at camp, Hospital visiting, Helping with five-a-side football, Football training, Housework, Car park marshalling, Cleaning workshops and garages.

South-West Lancashire

Assisting at youth club, Helping to run youth club, Supervision of festival, Supervising youth club activities, Marshalling duties at show, Helping with fun fair stalls, Helping to run club, Serving breakfast, Laundry, Washing dishes, Making and delivering maidens, Peeling potatoes, Mending windows, Cleaning windows, Chopping firewood, Hedge cutting, Planning funfair, Being Father Christmas at children's party, Grasscutting, Gardening, Painting, Decorating, Cleaning paintwork, Preparing railings for painting, Repairing wooden building, Repairing furniture, Court making, Spreading roof insulation, Washing walls, Labouring, Plastering, General duties, Various repairs, Digging ditches, Caring duties, Work in graveyard, Churchyard maintenance, Clearing paths, Clearing gardens, Making roads, Estates work, Restaining floor, Transporting ash to cellar, Reorganising community service workshop, Clearing workshop, Workshop maintenance, Preparing appeals literature, Preparing probation camp report, Cleaning equipment, Glazing, Digging, Moving building blocks, Play supervision, Supervision, Clearing rubbish, Making bats, Laying flags.

Durham

Snow clearance, Fence erection, Replacing fencing posts, Gardening, Laying lawns, Laying paths, Hedge cutting, Rubbish clearance, Assisting at sports meeting, Electrical repairs, Work with the elderly, Furniture removal, Decorating, Plastering, Painting, Cementing, River bank clearance, Building a rabbit hutch, Assisting handicapped children to swim, Cleaning windows, Flooring, Pruning trees, Landscaping gardens, Assisting at old age pensioners' concert, Typing, Tarmac stripping, Varnishing, Cooking, Serving in charity shop, Clerical work, Helping in children's playgroup, Taking children for a walk, Repairing toilet fittings, Visiting physically handicapped, Befriending patients, Assisting disabled archers, Assisting disabled at sports, Assisting at club for physically handicapped, Erecting tent for fete, Clearing bricks, Site clearance, Archaeological excavations, Overhaul and working on machinery at museum, Assisting disabled children to ride ponies, Helping in junior youth club, Window and ventilator repairing, Football pitch clearance, Repainting wheelchairs, Teak oiling, Demolishing work, Operating machinery at museum.

Kent

TV appearance, Refurbishing litter bins, Roofing, Carpentry, Fitting sink unit, Working in hospital, Renovating building, Laying footpaths, Moving furniture, Removing ceiling, Household repairs for blind, Glazing, Gardening, Paint scraping, Cleaning, Fitting lock for OAPs, Sawing and delivering logs, Laying foundations, Demolition, Repairing brickwork, Bricklaying, Furniture removal, Clearance, Painting and decorating, Painting and creosoting, Indoor repairs, Remooring barge, Plumbing, Signwriting, Assisting with playgroup for young children, Carpet laying, Building a rabbit hutch, Rubble clearance, Felling trees, Stacking concrete slabs, Helping in children's home, Nursing children,

Overhauling marine engine, Refitting guttering, Nursing and feeding handicapped children, Preparing timber, Blazing, Road repairs, Laying land drains, Moving stones, Sweeping and tidying hospital gardens, Cleaning, Driving, Serving and helping at old people's welfare group, Fixing handrail for old lady, Helping at youth club, Boxing tuition, Oasthouse conversion, Creosoting sail loft and fencing, Shipwrighting.

Shropshire

Teaching handicapped children to swim, Assisting blind handicapped children, Organising football for the handicapped, Taking handicapped shopping, Assisting with playgroup, Helping at hospital social, Taking handicapped to the fair, Landscaping, Gardening, Bricklaying, Demolition, Fence creosoting, General maintenance and repair work, Earth removal, Concreting fireproof pads for scouts, Brick stacking, Brick cleaning, Churchyard maintenance, Canal clearance, Painting, Fence painting, Constructing children's playground, Cycle repair, Selling flags for charity, Tree trimming, Helping at swimming clubs, General work at Franciscan College, Helping at school fete, Cooking, Mending toys, Mending furniture, Site clearance, Acetylene cutting, Road laying, Railway siding clearance, Railway siding rebuilding, Keeping tool store, Repairing canal banking, Whitewashing, Timber stacking, Noticeboard fixing, Dismantling museum cases, Workshop preparation, Exhibit collecting, Electrical wiring, Caravan painting, Caravan repairs.

Titles already published for the Home Office

Studies in the Causes of Delinquency and the Treatment of Offenders

1. Prediction Methods in Relation to Borstal Training
by Dr Herman Mannheim and Leslie T. Wilkins.

2. Time Spent Awaiting Trial
by Evelyn Gibson.

3. Delinquent Generations
by Leslie T. Wilkins.

4. Murder
by Evelyn Gibson and S. Klein.

5. Persistent Criminals
by W. H. Hammond and Edna Chayen.

6. Some Statistical and other Numerical Techniques for Classifying Individuals
by P. Macnaughton-Smith.

7. Probation Research. A Preliminary Report
by S. Folkard, K. Lyon, M. M. Carver, and E. O'Leary.

8. Trends and Regional Comparisons in Probation (England and Wales)
by Hugh Barr and E. O'Leary.

9. Probation Research. A survey of Group Work in the Probation Service
by H. Barr.

10. Types of Delinquency and Home Background. A Validation Study of Hewitt and Jenkins' Hypothesis
by Elizabeth Field.

11. Studies of Female Offenders
by Nancy Goodman and Jean Price.

12. The Use of the Jesness Inventory on a Sample of British Probationers
by Martin Davies.

13. The Jesness Inventory: Application to Approved School Boys
by Joy Mott.

Home Office Research Studies

1. Workloads in Children's Departments
by Eleanor Grey.

2. Probationers in their Social Environment
by Martin Davies.

3. Murder 1957 to 1968
by Evelyn Gibson and S. Klein.

4. Firearms in Crime
by A. D. Weatherhead and B. M. Robinson.

5. Financial Penalties and Probation
by Martin Davies.

5. Hostels for Probationers
by Ian Sinclair.

7. Prediction Methods in Criminology
by Frances H. Simon.

8. Study of the Juvenile Liaison Scheme in West Ham 1961 to 1965
by Marilyn Taylor.

9. Explorations in After-Care
by Ian Sinclair, Martin Silberman, Brenda Chapman and Aryeh Leissner.

10. A Survey of Adoption in Great Britain
by Eleanor Grey.

11. Thirteen-year-old Approved School Boys in 1962
by Elizabeth Field, W. H. Hammond and J. Tizard.

12. Absconding from Approved Schools
by R. V. G. Clarke and D. N. Martin.

13. An Experiment in Personality Assessment of Young Men Remanded in Custody
by Sylvia Anthony.

14. Girl Offenders Aged 17 to 20 years
by Jean Davies and Nancy Goodman.

15. The Controlled Trial in Institutional Research
by R. V. G. Clarke and D. B. Cornish.

16. A Survey of Fine Enforcement
by P. Softley.

17. An Index of Social Environment
by Martin Davies.

18. Social Enquiry Reports and the Probation Service
by Martin Davies.

19. Depression, Psychopathic Personality and Attempted Suicide in a Borstal Sample
by H. Sylvia Anthony.

20. The Use of Bail and Custody by London Magistrates' Courts Before and After the Criminal Justice Act 1967
by Frances Simon and Mollie Weatheritt.

21. Social Work in the Environment
by Martin Davies.

22. Social Work in Prison
by Margaret Shaw.

23. Delinquency amongst Opiate Users
by Joy Mott and Marilyn Taylor.

24. IMPACT. Intensive matched Probation and After-Care Treatment. Volume 1. The design of the probation experiment and an interim evaluation.
by M. S. Folkard, A. J. Fowles, B. C. McWilliams, W. McWilliams, D. D. Smith, D. E. Smith and G. R. Walmsley.

25. The Approved School Experience
by Anne B. Dunlop.

26. Absconding from Open Prisons
by Charlotte Banks, Patricia Mayhew and R. J. Sapsford.

27. Driving while Disqualified
by Sue Kriefman.

28. Some Male Offenders' Problems
Part I. Homeless offenders in Liverpool
by W. McWilliams.

Part II. Casework with short-time prisoners
by Julie Holborn.

H.M.S.O.

Government publications can be purchased from the Government Bookshops at the addresses listed on cover page iv (post orders to P.O., Box 569, London, S.E.1), or through any bookseller.

Printed in England for Her Majesty's Stationery Office by The Hillingdon Press, Uxbridge, Middlesex.
Dd. 506837 K00 2/75